Zimbabwe

A SURVEY BY THE

Africa Governance Monitoring and Advocacy Project (AfriMAP),
Open Society Initiative Southern Africa (OSISA) and
Open Society Institute Media Programme (OSIMP)

OPEN SOCIETY
FOUNDATIONS

Written by:
Dr Sarah Chiumbu (researcher), Jeanette Minnie (regional editor) and Hendrik Bussiek (editor-in-chief)

Published by:
Open Society Initiative for Southern Africa

ISBN: 978-1-920355-26-5
ISBN (Ebrary): 978-1-920489-66-3
ISBN (MyiLibrary): 978-1-920489-67-0
ISBN (Adobe PDF digital edition): 978-1-920489-68-7

For more information contact:
AfriMAP
President Place
1 Hood Ave/148 Jan Smuts Ave
Rosebank
South Africa

P.O. Box 678
Wits, 2050
Johannesburg
South Africa

www.afrimap.org
www.osisa.org

Layout and printing:
COMPRESS.dsl, South Africa

Distributed by
African Minds
4 Eccleston Place, Somerset West, 7130, South Africa
info@africanminds.co.za
www.africanminds.co.za

ORDERS:
African Books Collective
PO Box 721, Oxford OX1 9EN, UK
orders@africanbookscollective.com
www.africanbookscollective.com

Contents

Acronyms

ACHPR	African Commission on Human and Peoples' Rights
ACPD	African Community Publishing and Development Trust
AIPPA	Access to Information and Protection of Privacy Act
ANZ	Associated Newspapers of Zimbabwe
AU	African Union
BAZ	Broadcasting Authority of Zimbabwe
BBC	British Broadcasting Corporation
BSA	Broadcasting Services Act
CIO	Central Intelligence Office
CRI	Community Radio Initiative
CNAZ	Community Newspaper Association of Zimbabwe
CNP	Community Newspaper Publishing
CORAH	Community Radio Harare
CSO	Central Statistical Office
CZC	Crisis in Zimbabwe Coalition
EU	European Union
FAMWZ	Federation of African Media Women Zimbabwe
FCTZ	Farm Community Trust of Zimbabwe
GDP	Gross Domestic Product
GMB	Grain Marketing Board
GPA	Global Political Agreement
ICA	Interception of Communications Act
ICCPR	International Covenant on Civil and Political Rights
IMF	International Monetary Fund
ISP	internet service provider
ITU	International Telecommunication Union
LOMA	Law and Order (Maintenance) Act
MAZ	Media Alliance of Zimbabwe
MDC	Movement for Democratic Change
MIC	Media and Information Commission
MISA	Media Institute of Southern Africa
MMPZ	Media Monitoring Project of Zimbabwe
NCA	National Constitutional Assembly
OAU	Organisation of African Unity
OSA	Official Secrets Act
PIRF	Public Information Rights Forum

POSA	Public Order and Security Act
POTRAZ	Post and Telecommunications Regulatory Authority of Zimbabwe
SABC	South African Broadcasting Corporation
SADC	Southern African Development Community
STERP	Short Term Emergency Recovery Programme
SWRA	Short Wave Radio Africa
UNESCO	United Nations Educational, Scientific and Cultural Organisation
VMCZ	Voluntary Media Council of Zimbabwe
VoP	Voice of the People
VoIP	Voice over Internet Protocol
ZACRAS	Zimbabwe Association of Community Radio Stations
ZAMPS	Zimbabwe All Media Products Survey
ZANU	Zimbabwe African National Union
ZANU PF	Zimbabwe African National Union (Patriotic Front)
ZAPU	Zimbabwe African People's Union
ZAR	South African rand
ZBC	Zimbabwe Broadcasting Corporation
ZBH	Zimbabwe Broadcasting Holdings
ZCR	Zimbabwe Community Radio
ZCTU	Zimbabwe Congress of Trade Unions
ZEDC	Zimbabwe Electricity Distribution Company
ZESN	Zimbabwe Election Support Network
ZIANA	Zimbabwe Inter-Africa News Agency
ZINEF	Zimbabwe National Editors Forum
ZISPA	Zimbabwe Internet Service Providers Association
ZMC	Zimbabwe Media Commission
ZNLWVA	Zimbabwe National Liberation War Veterans Association
ZUJ	Zimbabwe Union of Journalists

Foreword

This report is the result of research that started in 2008 with the aim of collecting, collating and writing up information about regulation, ownership, access, performance as well as prospects for public broadcasting reform in Africa. The Zimbabwe report is part of an 11-country survey of African broadcast media. The main reason for conducting the research is to contribute to Africa's democratic consolidation.

Many African countries have made significant gains in building democratic systems of governance that are based on popular control of decision-making and in which citizens are treated as equals. Availability and access to information by a greater number of citizens is a critical part of a functioning democracy and a country's development. The role of a public broadcaster as a vehicle through which objective information and diverse perspectives are transmitted into the public domain cannot be overstated.

A number of countries are currently undertaking public broadcast media reforms that aim to improve service delivery and accountability to citizens. Such reforms draw from evolving African and global standards regarding media and broadcast media in particular. The survey instrument that was developed in consultation with media experts from Africa and other parts of the world is largely based on agreements, conventions, charters and declarations regarding media that have been developed at regional and continental levels in Africa.

The survey of broadcast media in Africa was initiated by two projects of the Open Society Institute (OSI), the Africa Governance Monitoring and Advocacy Project (AfriMAP) and the Media Programme, working with the African members of the Soros foundation network – in Southern Africa, the Open Society Initiative for Southern Africa (OSISA). The research was carried out by Dr Sarah Chiumbu who has worked in different capacities in media in Zimbabwe and currently teaches media studies at Wits University in Johannesburg. The report was edited by Jeanette Minnie, an international freedom of expression and media consultant. The project was overseen by an editor-in-chief, Hendrik Bussiek, a media consultant with extensive broadcasting experience in Africa and globally.

It is our hope that the research will clear some of the misconceptions about publ broadcasters. In its simplest definition a 'public broadcasting service' is a broadcaste that serves the public as a whole and is accountable to the public as a whole. Yet in most instances what is referred to as a public broadcaster is in fact a state broadcaster: this research aims to help the process of aiding the transformation of Africa's public broadcasters into media worthy of the name.

Ozias Tungwarara
Director, AfriMAP

Introduction

The survey on public broadcasting in Africa starts from the premise that development and democracy cannot thrive without open and free public space where all issues concerning people's lives can be aired and debated and which gives them room and opportunity to participate in decision-making. Nobel Prize laureate Amartya Sen describes democracy as 'governance by dialogue' and broadcasters are ideally placed to facilitate this dialogue by providing the space for it – if their services are accessible, independent, credible and open to the full spectrum of diverse views.

Following from this premise, the key objective of the survey is to assess whether and to what extent the various forms of broadcasting on our continent can and do create such a free public space, with special attention given to those services which call themselves 'public'. A total of 11 country reports look closely at the current status of broadcasting in Benin, Cameroon, Kenya, Mali, Mozambique, Namibia, Nigeria, South Africa, Uganda, Zambia and Zimbabwe.

While this survey may be unprecedented in its scope and depth, it does feed into ongoing discussions among broadcasters, civil society and politicians in Africa on the nature and mandate of genuine public broadcasting. Reform efforts are under way in a number of countries. And at least on paper there is already broad consensus on the need to open up the airwaves to commercial and community broadcasters and for state broadcasters to be transformed into truly public broadcasting services. The Declaration of Principles on Freedom of Expression in Africa adopted by the African Union's Commission on Human and Peoples' Rights in 2002, for example, says 'a State monopoly over broadcasting is not compatible with the right to freedom of expression' and demands that 'state and government controlled broadcasters should be transformed into public service broadcasters accountable to the public'. This document and other regional policy declarations serve as major benchmarks.

The facts, figures and informed assessments presented in the survey will, it is hoped, provide a nuanced picture of where broadcasting in Africa at present stands between 'His Master's Voice' of old and the envisaged public broadcasting service of the future. This information should provide a sound basis for advocacy work, both among decision-makers and civil society as a whole.

In the case of Zimbabwe the findings and recommendations of the country report come at a particularly timely juncture. The struggle for the opening up of the broadcasting spectrum and the transformation of the state-controlled Zimbabwe Broadcasting Corporation started years ago and scored a first major success in 2000 when the Supreme Court ruled that the state's monopoly of the airwaves violated the rights of freedom of expression and the freedom to impart information as stipulated in the Constitution of Zimbabwe. Unfortunately that judgement had no impact on the ground. This situation may change with the formation of an inclusive government of all major political parties in February 2009 which committed itself to 'liberalising the air waves', 'freeing the media' and 'ensuring that plural voices are heard through both electronic and print media'.

In order to assist the current, renewed efforts towards the development of a democratic media and broadcasting landscape in Zimbabwe, the research and editing team has made its findings, conclusions and recommendations successively available to media lobby groups as and when they were ready. Thus, some of the research results have already informed the formulation of media policies and proposed draft legislation or helped to highlight areas in particular need of reform even before completion of the survey.

The country report starts out with a comprehensive audit of existing media laws and legislation with an impact on freedom of expression and a critical in-depth assessment of broadcasting legislation. This had, somewhat surprisingly, never been done before and is meant to place the issues in context. Another first – and perhaps less surprisingly so – is the detailed study of the ZBC which makes up the bulk of the report. This research, too, had to start more or less from scratch and it proved to be extremely difficult to get information on the supposedly public broadcaster. The material compiled thus leaves some questions unanswered but still offers the most comprehensive overview of the ZBC available at present.

In September 2009, a draft report was publicly presented at a round table meeting in Zimbabwe's capital Harare which was attended by an impressive cross-section of civil society in general, media groups and political players. Participants discussed the findings, corrected assumptions or errors, debated and endorsed conclusions and recommendations and made a number of additions which were incorporated into the final version.

The researcher and editors are grateful to all the people in and outside Zimbabwe who contributed by sharing their information and insights and providing valuable feedback and constructive criticism.

Hendrik Bussiek

1

Country Facts

1 Historical background

Zimbabwe formally became an independent republic on 18 April 1980 after a long and turbulent history of colonisation by the British and white minority rule. In 1965, Ian Smith, prime minister of what was then the so-called self-governing British colony of Southern Rhodesia, unilaterally declared independence for the new country of Rhodesia, with himself continuing at the helm. In 1969 a new republican constitution was adopted, in which blacks were second-class citizens. These developments triggered a fiercely fought liberation war led by Robert Mugabe's Zimbabwe African National Union (ZANU) and Joshua Nkomo's Zimbabwe African People's Union (ZAPU). Negotiations between the warring parties and the British government in 1979 finally led to the Lancaster House Agreement which ended the war and instituted majority rule.

In founding elections held in February 1980 Mugabe's ZANU won with a landslide victory (63 per cent of the votes), followed by an even more favourable result in 1985 (77 per cent). Over the years Mugabe successfully consolidated his power, crushing political opposition and uprisings in the early 1980s in Matebeleland where thousands of lives were lost, changing the constitution in 1987 to give himself executive powers as president, and merging Nkomo's weakened ZAPU with his own party to create ZANU PF (Patriotic Front) in 1989. Elections in 1990 and 1995 returned ZANU PF[1] to power with a resounding 80.5 per cent and 81.4 per cent of the vote respectively, giving the party 118 out of the 120 elected seats in parliament.[2]

---

1 The spelling of ZANU PF has been sourced from the official website of ZANU PF – http://www.zanupf.org.zw/
2 African Elections Database, www.africanelections.tripod.com/zm

The first broad-based opposition party, the Movement for Democratic Change (MDC), was founded in 1999. Together with many members of a coalition of civil society groups, individuals and the Zimbabwe Congress of Trade Unions (ZCTU) it campaigned for a 'No' vote in a 2000 constitutional referendum. The new constitution proposed by Mugabe would have given the president even more powers but was rejected by 55 per cent of the voters – much to the surprise and dismay of the ruling party.

The thorny issue of land ownership re-emerged round about this time and quickly made it to the top of the national agenda. White Zimbabweans, making up less than 1 per cent of the population, still owned 70 per cent of all commercially viable farm land in the country. Mugabe introduced a compulsory land restitution and re-distribution programme which was highly controversial and marred by violence, and led to a sharp decline in agricultural exports and production.

ZANU PF won the 2000 elections to the National Assembly by a slender margin of 48.6 per cent to the MDC's 47 per cent – a result which was disputed by electoral observers. Subsequent elections saw slightly better results for ZANU PF and Mugabe and some levelling off of support for the opposition, but were increasingly marked by violence, evidence of vote-rigging and widely disputed results.

In March 2008 early 'harmonised' (both presidential and parliamentary) elections were held. By this time the opposition MDC had split, following a dispute over participation in the 2005 senate election, with the main formation headed by founder Morgan Tsvangirai (MDC-T) and the break-away group by Arthur Mutambara (MDC-M). Both groups together won 51.3 per cent (110 seats), with ZANU PF – for the first time – coming second at 45.9 per cent (99 seats) and one seat going to an independent candidate. In the contest between the two presidential candidates Tsvangirai won the first round with 47.9 per cent of the votes, with Mugabe trailing at 43.2. The MDC candidate withdrew from the second round a week before it was scheduled to take place, citing sustained violence against his party's supporters. The run-off election went ahead nevertheless with Mugabe as the only candidate. He won by an overwhelming 85.5 per cent, based on a voter turnout of 42 per cent,[3] and was sworn in for another term as president on 29 June.[4]

Following domestic and international pressure and the almost total collapse of the economy, ZANU PF and the two MDC formations entered into negotiations, mediated by Thabo Mbeki (the former South African president) on behalf of the Southern African Development Community (SADC). On 15 September 2008, Robert

---

3   CNN.com/world report published on 29 June 2008, citing the Zimbabwe Electoral Commission http://edition.cnn.
    com/2008/WORLD/africa/06/29/zimbabwe.sunday/index.html#cnnSTCText
4   Robert Mugabe received 2 150 269 votes, Morgan Tsvangirai 233 000; there were 131 481 spoiled ballots. Voter turnout
    was 42.37% (Source: Zimbabwe Electoral Commission).

Mugabe, Morgan Tsvangirai and Arthur Mutambara signed a so-called Global Political Agreement (GPA) to establish an 'inclusive' or transitional government. Under the agreement, Mugabe retained the presidency and Tsvangirai was to become prime minister – a position yet to be created under the constitution.

After five more months of negotiations Constitutional Amendment 19 was passed by parliament on 5 February 2009, implementing the terms of the GPA and paving the way for the formation of the inclusive government. On 11 February MDC-T leader Morgan Tsvangirai was sworn in as prime minister, alongside deputy prime ministers Arthur Mutambara (MDC-M) and Thokozani Khupe (MDC-T). In the following week, no less than 41 ministers and 20 deputy ministers were sworn into office.

With the inauguration of the new government economic recovery began to pick up slowly. The adoption of foreign currencies (mainly the US dollar and the South African rand), commonly referred to as the dollarisation of the economy, stopped hyperinflation and civil servants received 'allowances' in US dollars. Schools and hospitals managed to resume operations despite staff shortages and inadequate pay. All documented political detainees were released, although the whereabouts of several MDC supporters remains unknown. However, a number of new farm invasions and other alleged violations of the GPA has deterred full international engagement, resumption of robust donor support, and significant private investment. President Mugabe is alleged to be continuing to act as if he was the sole head of government without sharing powers as envisaged by the GPA, and MDC and ZANU PF rivals in government are contesting each other's authority.

2 Government

Zimbabwe has a presidential-parliamentary system with a president as head of state and government, elected by popular majority vote, and a prime minister. According to Constitutional Amendment 19 both 'shall exercise executive authority subject to the Constitution and the law'. The president is required to consult with the prime minister before the allocation of ministerial portfolios, commissions and other 'key appointments' (which are not clearly defined).

The government controls senior appointments in the public service, including the military and police, and the Public Service Commission is charged with making appointments at lower levels.

Parliament is bicameral and sits for a five-year term. The 210-member house of assembly is elected by voters in 210 constituencies. The second chamber is the senate, with 93 senators elected by ballot. Other senators include ten provincial governors, five presidential appointees, 16 chiefs elected by other chiefs, as well as the president and deputy president of the council of chiefs (traditional leaders).

Zimbabwe is divided into ten provinces, each administered by a provincial governor appointed by the president. Governors are assisted by a provincial administrator and representatives of several service ministries.

The judiciary is headed by the chief justice of the Supreme Court. Like the other justices, he or she is appointed by the President on the advice of the Judicial Service Commission.

According to Constitutional Amendment 19, a 'Select Committee of Parliament composed of representatives of the Parties' is tasked with drafting a new constitution for Zimbabwe to replace the much-amended 1979 version that brought the country to independence. To this end it is to form subcommittees 'composed of members of Parliament and representatives of Civil Society', hold 'public hearings' and 'consultations', convene 'All Stakeholders Conferences' to consult and brief stakeholders on drafts, and finally report back to parliament. The draft constitution as recommended by the Select Committee 'shall be submitted to a referendum'. In keeping with the agreed timetable the referendum must be held by July 2010.

3   Economic and social development

Population	13.3 million (United Nations, 2007)[*]
GDP per capita	US$ 340 (World Bank estimate 2006)
Real GDP growth rate	−14 per cent (IMF estimate 2008)
Average inflation rate	Hyperinflation was stopped by the introduction of hard currencies. The month-on-month inflation rate stood at 1.0 per cent in July 2009[**]
Literacy	91 per cent
Life expectancy	44 years (male), 43 years (female) (World Health Organisation 2006), down from 62 years in 1990
Main languages	English (official), Shona (76 per cent), Sindebele (18 per cent); minority languages include Venda, Shangani and Nambya

[*]   Reliable data are currently not available.
[**] Report published by *The Zimbabwe Times* on 20 August 2009, citing the Central Statistical Office of Zimbabwe
      http://www.thezimbabwetimes.com/?p=21505

The new Zimbabwean government faces an array of economic problems. Despite a stabilisation of prices as a result of dollarisation and a predicted growth of

4 per cent in 2009, great challenges – including a shortage of foreign exchange, unemployment commonly estimated at 90 per cent and supply shortages – remain to be addressed.

The dramatic state of affairs has various root causes, among them the land redistribution campaign which caused a decline in agricultural exports, especially tobacco, as well as in tourism; substantial pension payments to members of the Zimbabwe National Liberation War Veterans Association (ZNLWVA) in 1997 which led to a crash of the Zimbabwe dollar by 74 per cent; and Zimbabwe's involvement from 1998 to 2002 in the war in the Democratic Republic of the Congo (DRC) which drained hundreds of millions of dollars from the economy.[5]

Inflation rose from an annual rate of 32 per cent in 1998 to an unofficial and staggering high of 231 150 888 per cent by December 2008, with the government continuing to use the conservative figure of 231 000 per cent that had been recorded by the Central Statistical Office (CSO) in May 2008. Since the introduction of the US dollar and the South African rand in January 2009, the Zimbabwean dollar – in the words of Minister of Finance Tendai Biti – has 'died a natural death'.

President Mugabe has long accused the European Union (EU) and the United States of 'sabotage' through the imposition of 'illegal sanctions' which, he maintains, caused the decline of the Zimbabwean economy. However, these sanctions only target top government officials and ZANU PF figures by imposing travel and banking restrictions on them in the US and the EU. A more real impact on the economy – as the new government's Short Term Emergency Recovery Programme (STERP) pointed out in March 2009 – is made by 'measures taken against Zimbabwe, denying the country the right to access credit facilities from international financial institutions ... as well as denying Zimbabwean companies access to lines of credit.'[6]

The government's STERP clearly sets out the major economic and social challenges that the country faces:

> At the epicentre of the economic crisis have been unprecedented levels of hyper-inflation, sustained period of negative Gross Domestic Product (GDP) growth rates, massive devaluation of the currency, low productive capacity, loss of jobs, food shortages, poverty, massive de-industrialisation and general despondency.
> Since 2006, virtually all sectors recorded declines in output, with agriculture, manufacturing and mining estimated to have declined by 7.3%, 73.3% and 53.9% respectively in 2008.
> As a result, unemployment and poverty levels increased sharply. Ironically,

---

5   It is estimated that the country was spending more than US$1 million a day in 'defending' the DRC.
6   *Short Term Emergency Recovery Programme*, Harare, March 2009.

Zimbabwe's economic decline occurred at the time when most African countries were achieving reasonable annual growth rates averaging 4.8% and mainly driven by sound and sustained macroeconomic policies which contained annual inflation at low levels averaging 10%.

The impact of the above was to leave the state of the country's education sector, once the best in Africa, to very low deplorable conditions ... As the economic conditions worsened, a number of teachers left the country in search for better working conditions. For those who remained behind, the conditions of service would not allow teachers to report for duty regularly owing to unaffordability to meet transport costs, as well as other basic necessities.

The economic decline has resulted in a sharp decrease in funding for health in real terms. This has directly contributed towards an unprecedented deterioration of health infrastructure, loss of experienced health professionals, drug shortages and a drastic decline in the quality of public health services. Zimbabwe continues to experience a high burden of preventable diseases such as malaria, HIV and AIDS, tuberculosis, diarrhea diseases, maternal care, etc. Inadequate provision of safe water and sanitation has also been responsible for spreading water borne diseases, leading to avoidable cholera deaths in the urban centres.

Given successive years of drought and reduced agricultural capacity, a substantial number of persons have to be provided with humanitarian assistance. Everything being equal, Zimbabwe requires 2 million tonnes of maize and about 500 000 tonnes of wheat per year to feed its population. In the past few years we have failed to produce on average more than 20% of these requirements.

Add to that the need to rebuild the machinery of a functioning, democratic state – an independent judiciary, a professional, non-partisan civil service, a vibrant and engaged civil society – and it is clear that the inclusive, or any other new government, and the Zimbabwean people as a whole face a truly Herculean task.

4   Rule of law

The Global Political Agreement acknowledges in its preamble that:

the values of justice, fairness, openness, tolerance, equality, non discrimination and respect of all persons without regard to race, class, gender, ethnicity, language, religion, political opinion, place of origin or birth are the bedrock of our democracy and good governance.

The new government has a long way to go to entrench these values. In a report titled *False Dawn* the international non-governmental organisation Human Rights Watch stated in September 2009:[7]

> There is mounting evidence that the new government is failing or unwilling to end serious human rights violations, restore the rule of law, institute fundamental rights reforms, and chart a new political direction for the country. Despite commitments made by all parties, the new power-sharing government has not taken any significant steps to ensure justice for victims of abuses or hold perpetrators of human rights violations to account.

One of the reasons for the failure to establish the rule of law in Zimbabwe seems to be the unbalanced structure of the new government, with one party, ZANU PF, holding all security-relevant ministries such as Defence, Justice and State Security, and co-chairing Home Affairs.

The report blames both sides of the inclusive government for the precarious state of affairs:

> ZANU PF ... has shown at best negligible commitment and willingness to implement the far-reaching reforms envisioned in the GPA. At worst, ZANU PF's conduct has deliberately undermined efforts to restore the rule of law and accountable government in Zimbabwe. The MDC's lack of effective power and its desire to ensure the survival of the power-sharing government is severely inhibiting its ability to push for human rights reforms.

5 Media landscape

5.1 Print media

The press is dominated by pro-government newspapers published by the Zimbabwe Newspapers Group (Zimpapers). The company is majority-owned by government which holds 51.09 per cent of the shares, with Old Mutual (one of the biggest financial institutions in the country) holding 23.80 per cent and the remaining 25.11 per cent owned by private companies.[8]

---

7   Human Rights Watch, *False Dawn – The Zimbabwe Power-Sharing Government's Failure to Deliver Human Rights Improvements*, New York, 2009.

8   'Media Ownership in Zimbabwe' by Guthrie Munyuki and MISA-Zimbabwe. Available on http://www.kubatana.net/docs/media/misaz_media_ownership_zim_051130.pdf, accessed 13 October 2009.

Zimpapers publishes the dailies *The Herald*, with a circulation of 40 000,[9] and *The Chronicle* (22 300). In September 2009 it added a new tabloid to its stable – the *Harare-Metro/H-Metro* – in the face of vocal opposition from privately owned media houses and civil society organisations who saw this as an unfair move while other, new private publications were still battling to get registered, and a strong indication that government was intent on continuing to control large sections of the press.

Zimpapers also owns *The Manica Post* (12 000), a weekly paper based in the eastern parts of the country, two Sunday weeklies, *The Sunday Mail* (38 000) and *The Sunday News* (16 000), as well as two other weekly papers published in Shona and siNdebele respectively, *Kwayedza* (7000) and *Umthunywa* (5000).

In addition, there are ten local weeklies in various towns and districts of Zimbabwe, with a combined circulation of 41 200, owned by Community Newspaper Publishing (CNP), a division of the government-owned news agency, New Ziana.

Private publications came under severe pressure from 1999. A leading private daily, *The Daily News*, and its sister paper, *The Daily News on Sunday*, were banned and had to discontinue publication in September 2003 after a protracted legal battle with the government-controlled Media and Information Commission (MIC). Other independent papers to suffer the same fate include *The Tribune* and the *Weekly Times*, which were closed in 2003 and 2004 respectively.

The remaining private press is largely confined to three weeklies, *The Financial Gazette* (9000), *The Standard* (15 000) and *The Zimbabwe Independent* (22 000). Another newspaper, *The Zimbabwean*, is produced in London, printed in South Africa and distributed three times a week in Zimbabwe as an international publication with a circulation of 25 000 per edition.

The Financial Gazette is said to be owned by the governor of the Reserve Bank, Gideon Gono. *The Zimbabwe Independent* and *The Standard* are published by ZimInd Publishers (Pvt.) Ltd, which is majority owned by Trevor Ncube, the Zimbabwean owner of the South African based *Mail & Guardian*. *The Zimbabwean* is owned by Wilf Mbanga, the founding managing director of the former *Daily News*.

There are ten private local weeklies with a combined circulation of approximately 4000. They range in size between four and ten pages and are predominantly in English. These papers are organised by the Community Newspaper Association of Zimbabwe (CNAZ), which seeks to develop capacity among its members, both in terms of editorial and media business skills. Most of these privately owned papers operate on shoestring budgets and lack funding. Government has accused some of being tools of regime change and receiving donor money to write anti-Mugabe

---

9   All circulation figures mentioned in this report are self-reported and not independently verifiable.

propaganda.[10] According to research, however, 'a reading of these newspapers [shows they] are not generally engaged in any anti-Mugabe crusade, but simply articulate important issues occurring within their communities'.[11]

5.2 Broadcasting

Government retains its monopoly over broadcasting, with the Zimbabwe Broadcasting Corporation (ZBC) being the sole licenced service provider. The only alternative Zimbabwean voices on the airwaves are those broadcast for a few hours a day on short wave radio stations operated from abroad such as Voice of the People, SW Radio Africa, Studio 7 and Community Radio Zimbabwe. For more details see chapter three.

5.3 New ZIANA

The government has a 100 per cent controlling stake in New ZIANA Private Limited, formerly known as the Zimbabwe Inter-Africa News Agency (ZIANA). New ZIANA runs a news agency and provincial newspapers within the Community Newspaper Publishing (CNP) stable.

New ZIANA was intended to be at the centre of news collection and distribution in the country through various news exchange agreements with international news agencies. In recent years, however, most people and media organisations, including Zimpapers and the ZBC, have been turning to international news agencies instead of relying on the material offered by New ZIANA.[12]

New ZIANA failed to generate income by selling print and broadcasting stories to media outlets and is currently facing imminent collapse, barring a major intervention and rescue operation.

5.4 Internet news sites

According to a 2008 report by Internet World Stats,[13] Internet usage in Zimbabwe has grown by 165 per cent over the last three years, bringing the number of users to 1 351 000. Over the same period, Internet penetration (the percentage of people using the Internet) has gone up from 6.7 per cent to 10.9 per cent.[14]

---

10 Government spokesperson George Charamba quoted in the online publication *Zimdaily* on 28 March 2007.
11 All information in this section on privately owned local and district newspapers has been sourced from *Zimbabwe's 'Community' Newspapers*, a study conducted by the Media Monitoring Project of Zimbabwe (MMPZ) in 2007.
12 Sources inside Zimpapers and ZBC who do not want to be named.
13 Internet World Stats tracks Internet usage the world over, but data are usually estimates. Available on www. newzimbabwe.com
14 Ibid.

Broadband is available in Zimbabwe, but to a very limited number of users only due to its high cost and the unavailability of infrastructure.[15] Insufficient broadband capacity makes access to the Internet generally slow and expensive. Accessing television and radio broadcasting through the Internet is currently not a feasible option.

The most popular news websites according to the 2007 Zimbabwe All Media Products Survey (ZAMPS) are *ZimOnline* (South Africa based), *Zimdaily.com* (UK based), *The Zimbabwe Times* (USA based) and *NewZimbabwe.com* (UK based). *ZimOnline*, for example, is staffed by Zimbabweans and provides continually updated daily news services for African and international newspapers and broadcasters, other online news providers and general readers of its website and those on its e-mail subscription lists.

These websites owe their popularity to the keenness of Zimbabweans to obtain news other than that churned out by the national broadcaster. Many people in Zimbabwe access the Internet mainly because they want to communicate with their relatives in the diaspora through e-mail. This is the cheapest method of communication and even elderly people have learned to use it in order to stay in touch with their children who have left the country as a result of the economic downturn. The use of e-mail has in turn led to the discovery of the Internet and alternative sources of Zimbabwean news and information. To some extent the Internet has contributed to political communication between the citizenry, thereby fulfilling a need which is currently not addressed by public television or radio.

6   Brief history of broadcasting in Zimbabwe

Radio broadcasting in colonial Southern Rhodesia began in 1933, but it was not until 1941 that the first professional broadcaster was established.[16]

In 1948, Lusaka (the capital of Zambia – then Northern Rhodesia) became the focal point for broadcasting to African listeners in Northern Rhodesia, Southern Rhodesia and Nyasaland (today's Malawi), while Salisbury (today's Harare) became the centre for European broadcasting in the region. From 1950, African programmes were collected and packaged and sent to Lusaka for transmission.

In 1951 the Southern Rhodesian government set up a commission headed by Hugh Green (later to become the Director General of the British Broadcasting Corporation) to advise it on how broadcasting was to be run. The commission recommended the

---

15   Interview with Zimbabwe Online Marketing Manager Tiwonge Machiwenyika on 21 March 2008.
16   C. Mararike, 'A Historical Overview of Media and Political Change in Rhodesia', in: R. Zhuwarara et al (eds), *Media, Democratization and Identity*, University of Zimbabwe publishers, Harare, 1997. p. 57.

establishment of a broadcasting corporation, which was to be an independent statutory body. In 1958 the Federal Broadcasting Corporation came into operation, serving the Central African Federation of Southern and Northern Rhodesia and Nyasaland which had been formed by the colonial rulers in 1953. After the break-up of the Federation in 1963 separate corporations were established in the three territories and on 1 January 1964 the Rhodesia Broadcasting Corporation (RBC) came into existence.

At independence in 1980 the RBC became the Zimbabwe Broadcasting Corporation (ZBC). The corporation inherited not only old equipment but also a broadcasting system which had been controlled by the colonial and white minority governments and used as an effective tool to propagate their aims and keep subjects in their place as subjects.

The 1957 Broadcasting Act, which guaranteed the state a monopoly over broadcasting, was kept in place:

> No person other than the Corporation shall carry on a broadcasting service in the country. No person other than the Corporation ... shall operate a diffusion service ... otherwise than in accordance with the approval of the Minister or other consultation with the Posts Corporation.[17]

This monopoly was eventually challenged by the private company *Capital Radio* and declared unconstitutional in 2000 by the Supreme Court of Zimbabwe. The court ordered that the government formally end its monopoly by amending the law. In response the government hurriedly drafted the Broadcasting Services Presidential Powers (Temporary Measures) Bill, which became an Act in April 2001.

The Act sets up the Broadcasting Authority of Zimbabwe (BAZ) as a statutory regulator. Up to September 2009 it has not granted a single licence to a non-state broadcaster.

This is why private and community Zimbabwean radio stations are presently broadcasting from outside the country on short and medium wave.

---

17   Broadcasting Act, Section 27 and 28 (1) 1957, amended 1974.

2

Media Legislation and Regulation

1 International, continental and regional standards

1.1 United Nations

The following instruments of the United Nations are relevant to freedom of expression:

The Universal Declaration of Human Rights (adopted 1948)

The Universal Declaration is not a treaty that is ratified by states and thus legally binding. However, scholars now regard it as either having itself become international customary law or as a reflection of such law.[18] In either case the inclusion of freedom of expression in the declaration implies that even states that have ratified none of the relevant treaties are bound to respect freedom of expression as a human right.

Article 19 of the Declaration deals with the right to freedom of expression:

> Everyone has the right to freedom of opinion and expression; this right includes freedom to hold opinions without interference and to seek, receive and impart information and ideas through any media and regardless of frontiers.

---

18 See, for example, H. Hannum, 'The Status and Future of the Customary International Law of Human Rights: The Status of the Universal Declaration of Human Rights in National and International Law', *Georgia Journal of International and Comparative Law*, 287; H. J. Steiner, P. Alston and R. Goodman, *International Human Rights in Context: Law, Politics, Morals – Texts and Materials*, Oxford: Oxford University Press (third edition), 2007.

International Covenant on Civil and Political Rights (adopted 1976)

The International Covenant on Civil and Political Rights (ICCPR) is a treaty that elaborates on many of the rights outlined in the Declaration. Zimbabwe is a party to the ICCPR, having acceded to it in 1991. The Covenant's Article 19 declares:

1) Everyone shall have the right to hold opinions without interference;
2) Everyone shall have the right to freedom of expression; this right shall include freedom to seek, receive and impart information and ideas of all kinds, regardless of frontiers, either orally, in writing or in print, in the form of art, or through any other media of his choice.

The Windhoek Declaration on Promoting an Independent and Pluralistic African Press (adopted by the General Assembly of the UN Educational, Scientific and Cultural Organisation [UNESCO] in 1991)

UNESCO's Windhoek Declaration, like other non-treaty documents, has moral authority by representing a broad consensus of the international community on the detailed interpretation of the Universal Declaration and other relevant standards as they relate to the press in Africa. Article 9 of the Windhoek Declaration states:

(We) declare that
1) Consistent with Article 19 of the Universal Declaration of Human Rights, the establishment, maintenance and fostering of an independent, pluralistic and free press is essential to the development and maintenance of democracy in a nation, and for economic development.
2) By an independent press, we mean a press independent from governmental, political or economic control or from control of materials and infrastructure essential for the production and dissemination of newspapers, magazines and periodicals.
3) By a pluralistic press, we mean the end of monopolies of any kind and the existence of the greatest possible number of newspapers, magazines and periodicals reflecting the widest possible range of opinion within the community.

1.2 African Union

Zimbabwe is a member of the African Union (AU), whose Constitutive Act states that its objectives include the promotion of 'democratic principles and institutions, popular participation and good governance' (Article 3[g]).

The most important human rights standard adopted by the AU, or its predecessor, the Organisation of African Unity (OAU), is:

The African Charter on Human and Peoples' Rights (adopted 27 June 1981)

Zimbabwe acceded to the Charter in May 1986 and is thus bound by its provisions. The Charter's Article 9 on freedom of expression states:

- Every individual shall have the right to receive information.
- Every individual shall have the right to express and disseminate his opinions within the law.

The African Commission on Human and Peoples' Rights (ACHPR) is the body established under the Charter to monitor and promote compliance with its terms.

In November 2008, in a resolution on the situation in Zimbabwe, the Commission expressed its concern 'about the repeated human rights violations, in particular those against human rights defenders, women defenders and journalists' and requested the African Union and the Southern African Development Community (SADC) 'to take appropriate measures to cease all forms of violence against the media and human rights defenders ...'.[19]

Two other documents deal with issues of freedom of expression and information more specifically:

Declaration of Principles on Freedom of Expression in Africa

In 2002, the African Commission adopted this Declaration to provide a detailed interpretation for member states of the AU of the rights to freedom of expression outlined in the African Charter. It states in its Article I:

> Freedom of expression and information, including the right to seek, receive and impart information and ideas, either orally, in writing or in print, in the form of art, or through any other form of communication, including across frontiers, is a fundamental and inalienable human right and an indispensable component of democracy.
>
> Everyone shall have an equal opportunity to exercise the right to freedom of expression and to access information without discrimination.

---

19   Resolution 138/08 24 November 2008, accessed from www.achpr.org on 18 March 2009.

The Declaration goes on to say in Article II:

> No one shall be subject to arbitrary interference with his or her freedom of expression; and
> Any restrictions on freedom of expression shall be provided by law, serve a legitimate interest and be necessary in a democratic society.

The Declaration details how such freedom of expression should be realised. Of particular relevance to this study is the statement regarding public broadcasting (Article VI):

> State and government controlled broadcasters should be transformed into public service broadcasters, accountable to the public through the legislature rather than the government, in accordance with the following principles:
> - public broadcasters should be governed by a board which is protected against interference, particularly of a political or economic nature;
> - the editorial independence of public service broadcasters should be guaranteed;
> - public broadcasters should be adequately funded in a manner that protects them from arbitrary interference with their budgets;
> - public broadcasters should strive to ensure that their transmission system covers the whole territory of the country; and
> - the public service ambit of public broadcasters should be clearly defined and include an obligation to ensure that the public receive adequate, politically balanced information, particularly during election periods.

The document also states that freedom of expression 'places an obligation on the authorities to take positive measures to promote diversity' (Article II), that community and private broadcasting should be encouraged (Article V), and that broadcasting and telecommunications regulatory authorities should be independent and 'adequately protected against interference, particularly of a political or economic nature' (Article VII). The Declaration furthermore provides for freedom of access to information and states that 'the right to information shall be guaranteed by law' (Article IV).

African Charter on Democracy, Elections and Governance (2007)

This Charter, adopted by African heads of state in 2007, highlights the importance of access to information in a democracy. It states:

(State parties shall) (p)romote the establishment of the necessary conditions to foster citizen participation, transparency, access to information, freedom of the press and accountability in the management of public affairs. (Article 2[10])
State parties shall ... ensure fair and equitable access by contesting parties to state controlled media during elections. (Article 17[3])

For the time being, though, these remain noble goals. By September 2009, 29 countries had signed the Charter but only two had ratified it (Mauritania and Ethiopia), and the treaty had thus not yet entered into force (which requires 15 ratifications). Zimbabwe was not among the signatories.

1.3   Southern African Development Community (SADC)

Zimbabwe is a member of the Southern African Development Community (SADC). The treaty establishing the SADC provides that member states shall operate in accordance with principles that include respect for human rights, democracy, and the rule of law (Article 4[c]). In addition, the regional structure has adopted several protocols to the SADC treaty related to media and/or communications:

SADC Protocol on Culture, Information and Sport (adopted in 2000)
Article 17 of the Protocol outlines the following key objectives, amongst others:

- Co-operation and collaboration in the promotion, establishment and growth of independent media, as well as free flow of information;
- Development and promotion of local culture by increasing local content in the media;
- Taking positive measures to narrow the information gap between the rural and urban areas by increasing the coverage of the mass media;
- Encouragement of the use of indigenous languages in the mass media as vehicles of promoting local, national and regional inter-communication;
- Ensuring the media are adequately sensitised on gender issues so as to promote gender equality and equity in information dissemination.

Article 18 focuses on information policies, including committing member states to 'create (a) political and economic environment conducive to the growth of pluralistic media'.

Article 20 enjoins member states to take 'necessary measures to ensure the freedom and independence of the media', with 'independence of the media' being defined as 'editorial independence, whereby editorial Policy and decisions are made by the media without interference'.

Zimbabwe has not yet ratified this Protocol.

SADC Declaration on Information and Communication Technology (2001)

This Declaration focuses on telecommunications structures and promotes the creation of a three-tier system in each country with:

> Government responsible for a conducive national policy framework, independent regulators responsible for licensing, and a multiplicity of providers in a competitive environment responsible for providing services. (Article 2[a][i])[20]

Although the Declaration does not have the same legal force as a protocol, all member countries (including Zimbabwe) have made a commitment in adopting it to abide by its provisions.

1.4 Other documents

African Charter on Broadcasting (2001)

This Charter was adopted by media practitioners and international media and other human rights organisations at a UNESCO conference to celebrate ten years of the Windhoek Declaration. Although it has not been endorsed by any inter-state structures, it represents a consensus of leading African and other international experts on freedom of expression and the media.

The Charter specifies, amongst other things, that there should be a three-tier system of broadcasting (public, private and community), demands that '(a)ll state and government controlled broadcasters should be transformed into public service broadcasters', and states that regulatory frameworks should be based on 'respect for freedom of expression, diversity and the free flow of information and ideas'.

2. The Constitution of Zimbabwe

The right to freedom of expression is guaranteed in Article 20 of the Constitution of Zimbabwe, which states in its subsection 1 that:

---

20 http://www.sadc.int/key_documents/declarations/ict.php

Except with his own consent or by way of parental discipline,[21] no person shall be hindered in the enjoyment of his freedom of expression, that is to say, freedom to hold opinions and to receive and impart ideas and information without interference and freedom from interference with his correspondence.

Subsection 2 then provides that freedom of expression can be limited for a number of reasons:

Nothing contained in or done under the authority of any law shall be held to be in contravention of subsection (1) to the extent that the law in question makes provision –

a) in the interests of defence, public safety, public order, the economic interests of the State, public morality or public health;

b) for the purpose of –

i) protecting the reputations, rights and freedoms of other persons or the private lives of persons concerned in legal proceedings;

ii) preventing the disclosure of information received in confidence;

iii) maintaining the authority and independence of the courts or tribunals or Parliament;

iv) regulating the technical administration, technical operation or general efficiency of telephony, telegraphy, posts, wireless broadcasting or television or creating or regulating any monopoly in these fields;

v) in the case of correspondence, preventing the unlawful dispatch therewith of other matter; or

c) that imposes restrictions upon public officers.

Some of these exclusions are rather vague, using undefined phrases such as 'public order', 'economic interests' and 'public morality'. The provision that the right to freedom of expression may be limited by 'restrictions upon public officers' is extremely wide and creates a 'constitutional' avenue for the operations of the public service to be shrouded in secrecy.

The same subsection also provides that a law restricting freedom of expression is not permissible 'so far as that provision or, as the case may be, the thing done under the authority thereof is shown not to be reasonably justifiable in a democratic society'.

This section of the Constitution provides much weaker protections than those spelled out by the African Commission in the Declaration of Principles on Freedom of

---

21 This provision is peculiar and seems to be unique to the Constitution of Zimbabwe. It is not clear what is meant by 'parental discipline'.

Expression in Africa in its Article 2(2): 'Any restrictions on freedom of expression shall be provided for by law, serve a legitimate interest and be necessary in a democratic society.'

For a restriction to be merely 'reasonably justifiable in a democratic society' is a far less stringent condition than for it to be 'necessary in a democratic society'. Moreover, the wording of the Constitution means that an individual seeking to assert the right to freedom of expression bears the burden of proving that a particular restriction is not justifiable, rather than the burden resting with the state to demonstrate to a court that the restrictions are justifiable.

Article 22 of the Constitution guarantees freedom of movement and thus, arguably, that of expression by means of demonstrations, but makes it possible to impose restrictions 'in the interests of defence, public safety, public order, public morality or public health'. In the 17th Amendment to the Constitution passed in September 2005, lawmakers added more reasons for such limitations: 'national interest', 'public interest' and 'economic interests of the state'.

Despite the general guarantee of freedom of expression on paper in the Constitution, the vast majority of people in Zimbabwe do not feel free to express their views. The African Media Barometer, a self-assessment instrument of media and civil society representatives, summarised the situation in January 2008 as follows:

> The atmosphere in Zimbabwe is not conducive to free expression. People voice their opinions freely only within their own group and often consider carefully where they are, who they are with and what they say under the circumstances. In rural Zimbabwe there is fear of victimisation and fear of disappearance, torture and violence when one expresses oneself.
>
> Security is everywhere and repression has become a norm which people have accepted. They fear being branded 'infidels' if they disagree with the views of officialdom and so become subservient to the political status quo: 'You can't even talk about the President's age'.
>
> Fear is further instilled by bloody images of activists, lawyers, opposition party members and ordinary citizens being assaulted by the police and the militia published in newspapers and broadcast by TV.
>
> Apart from the few alternative media which are difficult to access, there are no channels to express opinions publicly. As a result politicians are removed from what people think. Government communicates its policies through the various media under its control (Zimpapers, Zimbabwe Broadcasting Holdings) but citizens do not have the same access to these media when they want and need to express themselves.

This constraint on free expression is not confined to political issues. Every issue in Zimbabwe is seen as being a political issue with a political meaning. People are generally afraid to talk and this culture of fear permeates everything. In the courts, there are certain issues that lawyers cannot talk about because they are off limits. Politicians and policy-makers are even more restricted than the average citizens, as they cannot openly express their views: they make totally different statements on one and the same issue depending on whether they are in private or in public.

At universities, traditionally the hotbed of free debate, lecturers are often afraid to include certain contentious topics in their course outlines or comment on them. This 'culture of self-censorship' is described as widespread and universal amongst Zimbabweans. Equally, students no longer freely debate issues without fear.[22]

Space for freedom of expression in the media was severely restricted after the authorities closed down the Associated Newspapers of Zimbabwe (ANZ), publishers of the mass circulation *The Daily News* and *The Daily News on Sunday*, on 12 September 2003. This was without doubt the most significant blow to freedom of expression since independence. The only independent daily newspaper in the country had been a constant thorn in the side of the government, exposing its abuses and providing a platform for political voices other than those of the ruling party.

The closure of *The Daily News* was followed in 2005 by the closure of the weekly *The Tribune*, another independent newspaper, and *The Weekly Times*, a paper based in Bulawayo.

From 2005 to 2007, the harassment of journalists practising in Zimbabwe increased dramatically. According to the Media Institute of Southern Africa (MISA) Zimbabwe, more than 50 journalists were intimidated by state agents or imprisoned during this period after writing stories or publishing pictures that were deemed to be critical of the government.[23] Harassment of journalists continued even after some relaxation in media laws in December 2007 (see below). The campaign of repression carried on, even as regional leaders were working to establish dialogue between the ZANU PF government and the then opposition. The security forces persisted with arbitrary arrests, abductions, torture and other abuses, including beatings with whips and cables, suspension and electric shocks, to repress civil and political freedoms. 2007 and 2008 were the worst years for Zimbabwe's human rights defenders, who include journalists and the general public.

Following the signing of the 15 September 2008 Global Political Agreement, MISA-

---

22 African Media Barometer Zimbabwe Report 2008, indicator 1.2, accessed from www.fesmedia.org.na
23 MISA, *AIPPA Five Years On*, 2007, available on www.zimbabwejournalists.com/uploaddocs/AIPPA

Zimbabwe continued to record threats made against independent journalists in the state controlled media.

3. General media laws and regulations

3.1 Access to Information and Protection of Privacy Act (AIPPA)

The Access to Information and Protection of Privacy Act, commonly referred to as AIPPA, was passed by parliament on 31 January 2002 and signed into law by President Mugabe on 15 March 2002. It has been amended twice: on 13 October 2003 and 18 December 2007 (see more details below).

AIPPA, as it stands presently, establishes the Zimbabwe Media Commission (ZMC) and gives this body a wide range of regulatory powers over the media. The ZMC comprises a chairperson and eight other members. They are appointed by the president from a list of 12 nominees submitted by parliament's Committee on Standing Rules and Orders.

The functions of the ZMC are 'to uphold and develop the freedom of the press', as well as 'to promote and enforce good practice and ethics in the press, print and electronic media, and broadcasting' and to ensure that the people of Zimbabwe have 'equitable and wide access to information'. The ZMC has the power of registering mass media and news agencies, investigating complaints against media persons and services and reviewing decisions of public bodies regarding access to information.

The minister of information and publicity sets the term of office, as well as other terms and conditions of office, including allowances, appoints both the chair and the vice-chair, and may remove a member on a number of grounds, some of them quite vague (for example, where the member has conducted him- or herself in a manner which 'renders him unsuitable' – Fourth Schedule, pursuant to Article 40 [3]).

The ZMC has broad investigative powers and, as detailed below, the power to impose severe sanctions, including the termination of a media outlet's registration.

AIPPA also establishes a statutory Media Council, which is appointed by the ZMC and chaired by a one of its members. The Council consists of 12 other members, representing and nominated by associations of stakeholders in the following sectors: two members representing journalists; two representing advertisers and advertising agencies; representatives of mass media trainers, churches, business people, trade unions, women's groups, youth groups, the legal profession and tertiary educational institutions.

The various associations must 'in the opinion of the Commission be fairly representative' of their respective sector. If any association fails or refuses to submit nominations, the ZMC will appoint a person of their own choice. As the media in Zimbabwe had established their own self-regulatory media council before this statutory body was introduced (see below), it is not surprising that the state body is not recognised by a number of associations expected to nominate members. In practice, the government therefore both appoints the members of the ZMC and determines the composition of the Media Council.

On 5 June 2009, the parliamentary Committee on Standing Rules and Orders placed an advert in *The Herald* calling on Zimbabweans to apply for appointment to serve as commissioners on a number of independent commissions, among them the ZMC, as provided for in Sections 100(b)(k)(n)(r) of the Constitution. On 3 August, interviews with 27 candidates were held, with 12 being nominated to the president, who is to make the final selection of nine people to sit on the ZMC (more details on this in chapter nine).

The Media Council is supposed to work with the ZMC to develop and enforce a code of conduct and ethics to be observed by all journalists and mass media services and also, if so required by the ZMC, to deal with complaints against mass media services and journalists. In the event of a breach of the code the Council will recommend a penalty for imposition by the Commission. Penalties include fines, payment of the expenses incurred by the Council and Commission, cancellation of mass media service registration and publication of apologies or corrections in the case of 'injurious allegations'.

All these provisions do not comply with the Declaration of Principles on Freedom of Expression in Africa which says in its Articles IX(2) and (3):

> Any regulatory body established to hear complaints about media content, including media councils, shall be protected against political, economic or any other undue interference. Its powers shall be administrative in nature and it shall not seek to usurp the role of the courts.
> Effective self-regulation (of the media) is the best system for promoting high standards in the media.

3.2 Registration of mass media

AIPPA requires all 'mass media owners' who 'carry on the activities of a mass media service' to obtain a certificate of registration from the ZMC (Section 66). 'Mass media' is defined in the Act as 'any service, medium or media consisting in the transmission of voice, visual, data or textual messages to an unlimited number of persons, and includes an advertising agency, publisher or ... a news agency or broadcasting licensee'.

The registration fee is set by the minister of information and publicity, who is given broad discretion to apply higher fees to certain types of media services (Section 70). According to Section 65 it is also up to the minister to allow for foreign ownership in specific cases: The 'Minister may at his or her absolute discretion ... permit the Commission to register a mass media service approved by the Minister in which the controlling interest or a portion thereof is held by persons who are not citizens of Zimbabwe.'

Individuals who operate mass media services without a registration certificate are guilty of an offence and may be sentenced 'to imprisonment for a period not exceeding eighteen months' or payment of a fine.

The ZMC is given broad powers to terminate or suspend the activities of a mass media service upon upholding a complaint against it or for breach of the law. Section 71 says:

> ... the Commission may, whether on its own initiative or upon receipt of a complaint made by any interested person against the mass media service, suspend or cancel the registration certificate of a mass media service if, after due inquiry, it finds that –
>
> a) the registration certificate was issued through fraud or there was a fraudulent misrepresentation by the mass media owner concerned; or
>
> b) the registration certificate was issued through a material misrepresentation and the Commission has obtained a court order confirming the suspension or cancellation of the registration certificate of a mass media service; or
>
> c) a mass media service concerned does not publish any mass media products within twenty-four months from the date of registration; or
>
> d) the mass media service concerned has been convicted of a repeated contravention of section 76, 77, 78(2) or 89.

According to Section 76 a mass media service shall send free deposit copies of a periodical to the Commission and to the National Archives.

Section 77 says that:

> A mass media service shall be obliged to publish, free of charge and in the prescribed manner a decision of a court or the Commission pertaining to its mass media service that has come into effect, if it is a newspaper, on the front page or centrespread and if it is electronic media, three times during prime time.

Section 78(2) says that:

> Any person or journalist who in any manner holds himself or herself out as an
> accredited journalist without being so accredited shall be guilty of an offence and
> liable to a fine ... or to imprisonment for a period not exceeding two years or to both
> such fine and such imprisonment.

Section 89 deals with the right of reply:

> A person or organisation in respect of whom a mass media service has published
> information that is not truthful or impinges on his rights or lawful interests shall
> have a right of reply in the same mass media service at no cost to him, and the reply
> shall be given the same prominence as the offending story.

News agencies are also required to obtain a registration certification, with similar consequences in case of any breaches (Section 74).

Section 42D(c) gives the Commission – on the recommendation of the Media Council – the power to cancel the registration of a mass media service if it 'has breached the code more than once', this being the 'code of conduct and ethics' developed by the Commission.

The requirement for publications to register with a government controlled body (which can also de-register them) falls foul of international guarantees. As the three specialised international bodies mandated to protect freedom of expression – the United Nations Special Rapporteur on Freedom of Opinion and Expression, the Organisation for Security and Cooperation in Europe Representative on Freedom of the Media and the Organisation of American States Special Rapporteur on Freedom of Expression – stated in a Joint Declaration of 18 December 2003:

> Imposing special registration requirements on the print media is unnecessary
> and may be abused and should be avoided. Registration systems which allow for
> discretion to refuse registration, which impose substantive conditions on the print
> media or which are overseen by bodies which are not independent of government
> are particularly problematical.[24]

---

24 International Mechanisms for Promoting Freedom of Expression, *Joint Declaration by the UN Special Rapporteur on Freedom of Opinion and Expression, the OSCE Representative on Freedom of the Media and the OAS Special Rapporteur on Freedom of Expression*, see 'International experts condemn curbs on freedom of expression and control over media and journalists', United Nations, 18 December 2003.

The system established by AIPPA, overseen by the government-controlled Commission, is clearly designed to enable state control over the media in the country.

This control is further strengthened by the short registration period of five years. This means that privately owned media companies have no financial security of tenure in relation to their investments, and stand to lose these should the state close down their operations and confiscate their assets.

3.3   Accreditation of journalists

AIPPA was amended in December 2007 to scrap the compulsory accreditation of journalists with the state-controlled Media and Information Commission. But the amended act still contains a number of provisions regarding accreditation. Section 79 says:

a)   A mass media service or news agency shall make a block application or individual applications for accreditation in terms of this section on behalf of all or any journalists employed by it on a full-time basis.

b)   A part-time or freelance journalist may, if he or she so wishes, make application on his or her own behalf for accreditation in terms of this section.

c)   Subject to subsection (4), no journalist shall be accredited who is not a citizen of Zimbabwe, or is not regarded as permanently resident in Zimbabwe by virtue of the Immigration Act [Chapter 4:02].

d)   A journalist who is not a citizen of Zimbabwe, or is not regarded as permanently resident in Zimbabwe by virtue of the Immigration Act [Chapter 4:02], may be accredited for any period specified by the Commission not exceeding sixty days: Provided that the Commission may, for good cause shown or for the purpose of enabling the journalist to work for the duration of any event he or she is accredited to cover, extend the period by a specified number of days.

Accredited journalists receive a press card which allows them:

a)   to visit Parliament and any public body ...;

b)   to be given prior access or privileged access to records to which access is permitted in terms of this Act or to such other records or documents as may be prescribed;

c)   to attend any national event ...;

d)   to attend, as of right, and notwithstanding any reservation of the right of admission ..., any public event ...;

e) to make recordings with the use of audio-video equipment, photography and cine-photography ... for the purposes of paragraphs (a), (b), (c) and (d).

According to section 42D(a) of the amended AIPPA, the Commission – on the recommendation of the Media Council – has the power to 'do one or more of the following':

iii) suspending for a specified period not exceeding three months the accreditation of the journalist; or

iv) imposing such conditions as it deems fit subject to which he or she shall be allowed to practise; or

v) deleting his or her name from the roll of journalists [i.e. withdrawing the accreditation] ...

These sanctions can be imposed if a journalist 'abuses his or her journalistic privilege' in a number of ways spelt out meticulously in Section 80(1):

A journalist who abuses his or her journalistic privilege by publishing –

a) information which he or she intentionally or recklessly falsified in a manner which –

i) threatens the interests of defence, public safety, public order, the economic interests of the State, public morality or public health; or

ii) is injurious to the reputation, rights and freedoms of other persons; or

b) information which he or she maliciously or fraudulently fabricated; or

c) any statement –

i) threatening the interests of defence, public safety, public order, the economic interests of the State, public morality or public health; or

ii) injurious to the reputation, rights and freedoms of other persons; in the following circumstances –

A. knowing the statement to be false or without having reasonable grounds for believing it to be true; and

B. recklessly, or with malicious or fraudulent intent, representing the statement as a true statement;

shall be guilty of an offence and liable to a fine ... or to imprisonment for a period not exceeding two years.

3.4 Voluntary self-regulation of the media

Media practitioners and organisations first tried to launch a Media Council in 1995. Following the examples of their peers in the southern African region, they sought to set up a self-regulatory body to ensure compliance with professional standards and ethics of journalism and to pre-empt any state attempt to set up a statutory, that is, government-controlled body. However, with freedom of expression still taken for granted in Zimbabwe at the time there was no real sense of urgency and the initiative collapsed in 1997.

As tensions increased between the state and the media the same groups undertook a second attempt in 1999 but were stopped in their tracks the following year because the then minister of information did not allow state media to take part in the formation of such a body. The process again ground to a halt.

When the Access to Information and Protection of Privacy Act (AIPPA) established a Media and Information Commission with the power to register newspapers and journalists, the idea of self-regulation resurfaced but it took five years for the new initiative to bear fruit.

On 8 June 2007 a self-regulatory Media Council of Zimbabwe was officially launched by the Media Alliance of Zimbabwe (MAZ), a grouping that comprises the Media Monitoring Project of Zimbabwe (MMPZ), the Zimbabwe Union of Journalists (ZUJ), MISA-Zimbabwe and the Zimbabwe National Editors Forum (ZINEF). The MMPZ publishes weekly reports on the performance of the media, the ZUJ represents all journalists operating in the country, both in the private and state media, and ZINEF's members are the editors of both state and non-state Zimbabwean publications and broadcast media that operate within and from outside of the country. The Voluntary Media Council also enjoys the backing of the Federation of African Media Women Zimbabwe (FAMWZ).

Initially journalists and editors working for the state media endorsed the concept of a voluntary media council and the code of ethics, but they later had to withdraw, obviously following pressure 'from above'. MISA, the ZUJ and MMPZ have frequently been branded as organisations of 'regime change activists' by the Zimbabwean government.

After the amendments to AIPPA in December 2007 which established a statutory 'Media Council of Zimbabwe', it was decided to change the name of the self-regulatory body to the Voluntary Media Council of Zimbabwe (VMCZ) to avoid confusion.

With a lot of preparatory work and fundraising to be done under the difficult conditions pertaining in the country it took nearly another two years before the VMCZ was actually able to start its operations on 1 February 2009.

A code of ethics had been developed before the launch by the four founding members and the administrative structure of the VMCZ was put in place. In September 2009, its board comprised 14 members, seven public and seven media representatives appointed by the founding members. One of the 14 positions had been left vacant to allow for the editors of state-controlled publications to come on board should they decide to take up their seat.

A Media Complaints Committee, comprising three legal practitioners appointed by the board, has been established to adjudicate complaints from the public, using the code of ethics as a basis. Where applicable, media houses that subscribe to the VMCZ can be ordered by the Committee to publish corrections. Because the state media are not (yet) part of the structure, the Committee cannot officially adjudicate cases involving these media houses, but from time to time there are unofficial talks with state editors behind closed doors on complaints it has received.

The VMCZ is seeking to extend the scope of its work beyond adjudication to monitoring, research and the training of media practitioners on ethics and professionalism based on the issues and problem areas highlighted in the course of the body's adjudication and monitoring processes. One of the hurdles for the VMCZ is the fact that there are not many professional media trainers left in the country. The Council intends working with various SADC regional and international training institutions to fill this gap and to train editors as trainers.

4 Other laws with an impact on media and freedom of expression

In addition to the state-controlled system of media regulation, a wide range of other laws, some of them long-standing, some more recently introduced, provide the framework for government to limit freedom of expression and of the media in Zimbabwe.

4.1 Public Order and Security Act (POSA)

The Public Order and Security Act (POSA) was enacted on 10 January 2002, just before the presidential elections of that year, and amended in December 2007. It is largely a reincarnation of the Law and Order (Maintenance) Act (LOMA) of the 1960s. LOMA was widely used by the Rhodesian authorities to suppress civil dissent, and many nationalists, including President Robert Mugabe, were victims of this repressive legislation and detained for periods of up to more than ten years.

POSA was condemned by lawyers, human rights activists and journalists on the grounds that it contained several of the anti-democratic features of LOMA. For instance, Section 5 deals with 'subverting constitutional government' and says in subsection 2:

> Any person who, whether inside or outside Zimbabwe –
> a)   organises or sets up or advocates, urges or suggests the organisation or setting up of, any group or body with a view to that group or body –
>   i)   overthrowing or attempting to overthrow the Government by unconstitutional means; or
>   ii)   taking over or attempting to take over Government by unconstitutional means or usurping the functions of the Government of Zimbabwe; or
>   iii) coercing or attempting to coerce the Government;
>   or
> b)   supports or assists any such group or body in doing or attempting to do any of the things described in subparagraphs (i), (ii) or (iii) of paragraph (a);
> shall be guilty of an offence and liable to imprisonment for a period not exceeding 20 years without the option of a fine.

Public gatherings are also restricted. Section 27 of POSA empowers the 'regulating authority', the police, to prohibit all public gatherings within an area for up to three months, where they believe 'on reasonable grounds' that this will be necessary to 'prevent public disorder'. A good example of this was during the period before the 29 March 2008 elections when the police banned all political rallies in urban areas for four weeks, giving as their reason that there would be violence between ZANU PF and the MDC. However, ZANU PF went ahead with their campaigns in the urban areas despite the ban, while the MDC were not allowed to do so until two days before the election.

Section 27A prohibits gatherings in the vicinity of parliament, a court or any protected place or area declared as such in terms of the Protected Areas and Places Act [Chapter 11:12] unless permission for such gatherings is given by the speaker, chief justice, judge president or responsible authority of the protected place, as the case may be.

4.2 Criminal Law (Codification and Reform) Act 2004

The Criminal Law (Codification and Reform) Act was signed into law on 2 June 2004 and amended in March 2007. It introduced harsher penalties than those provided for under POSA and AIPPA. The law was adopted to further restrict freedom of expression and shield the president from public and media scrutiny.

Section 31(a) of the Act makes it an offence:

> ... for anyone inside or outside Zimbabwe to publish or communicate to any other person a statement which is wholly or materially false with the intention or realising that there is real risk or a possibility of any of the following:
>
> i)   Inciting or promoting public disorder or public violence or endangering public safety;
>
> ii)   Adversely affecting the defence or economic interests of Zimbabwe;
>
> iii)   Undermining public confidence in a law enforcement agency, the Prison Service or the Defence Forces of Zimbabwe;
>
> iv)   Interfering with, disrupting or interrupting any essential service.

An offence will still have been committed even if the publication or communication does not result in any of the envisaged scenarios.

Section 31(b) of the Act deals with issues extracted from Section 80 of AIPPA, namely the publication or communication of falsehoods. Under AIPPA, once convicted, a person is liable to two years imprisonment or a fine. In terms of the Codification Act a convicted offender under Section 31(b) can be jailed for a term of up to 20 years.

Section 33 of the Codification Act deals with 'undermining the authority of or insulting the President'. It prohibits the making, publicly and intentionally, of any false statement (including an act or gesture) about or concerning the president or acting president if the person knows or realises that there is a risk or possibility of engendering feelings of hostility towards or causing hatred, contempt or ridicule of him, whether in his official or personal capacity.

It is also an offence to make an abusive, indecent, obscene or false statement about the president, whether in his official or personal capacity. POSA imposes a fine or a one year jail term or both. The Codification Act raises the fine while the prison term remains the same.

4.3   Official Secrets Act (OSA)

The Official Secrets Act (OSA) is a pre-independence statute dating back to 1970 (and amended in 2004) that seeks to limit what official information can be made public. The Act prohibits communication of any official information by any civil servant. Communication of such information by anyone whom state officials may have entrusted with it in confidence is also a crime. Under the Act, it is an offence to communicate official information unless authorised to do so by a competent authority. However, the Act does not say which authority can authorise the disclosure of official information.

While the act is mainly aimed at state employees, some of its provisions relate to and affect the general public, journalists in particular. Under the heading 'Espionage' Section 3(c) says:

> Any person who, for any purpose prejudicial to the safety or interests of Zimbabwe
> – obtains, collects, records, publishes or communicates to any person – ...
>
>   ii)   any model, article, document or other information which is calculated to
>   be or which might or is intended to be useful directly or indirectly to the
>   enemy;
>
> shall be guilty of an offence and liable to imprisonment for a period not exceeding
> twenty-five years.

'Enemy' is defined as a 'hostile organisation' which is declared as such by the president.

4.4 Defamation legislation

Zimbabwean law contains provisions for both civil and criminal defamation.

The offence of civil defamation is based on Article 20(1)(b)(i) of the Constitution which lists 'protecting the reputations, rights and freedoms of other persons or the private lives of persons concerned in legal proceedings' as one of the grounds on which freedom of expression may be limited. According to media law experts Tendai Biti and Geoffrey Feltoe, it 'is no defence that the publisher of a defamatory statement had no intention to defame; that the publisher defamed the plaintiff by mistake; that the publisher genuinely believed the statement to be true; or that, even if the statement was indeed false and defamatory, it was in the public interest to publish the information.' In all such cases the 'burden is on the defendant to prove the truth of the statements published, and this is often particularly difficult in cases where the plaintiff is a high-ranking government official and where witnesses may be unwilling to come forward and testify.' Civil defamation actions 'or the threat of such actions, are frequently used by public figures and government officials as a way of inhibiting reporting by the press.'[25] For instance, between 2001 and 2003 alone then Minister of Information and Publicity Jonathan Moyo filed more than 20 cases of defamation against *The Zimbabwe Independent*.[26]

---

25 T. Biti and G. Feltoe, 'Media Law in Zimbabwe' (undated), accessed 24 March 2009 from www.fxi.org.za/pages/
    Publications/Medialaw/zim-fina.htm
26 Interview with G. Feltoe, University of Zimbabwe law lecturer, 10 November 2008 .

Civil defamation arrests still continued after the formation of the inclusive government in February 2009. In May, *Zimbabwe Independent* editors Vincent Kahiya and Constantine Chimakure were charged under Section 31 of the Criminal Law (Codification and Reform) Act, which criminalises the communication of statements that are likely to undermine public confidence in law enforcement agents. According to the provisions of this section, such offences attract a maximum sentence of imprisonment for 20 years. The charge arose from a story published in the paper in early May titled 'CIO, police role in activists' abduction revealed'. The two journalists appeared in court on 9 July, where their lawyer asked that their case be referred to the Supreme Court to challenge the constitutionality of Section 31 of the Criminal Law (Codification and Reform) Act. The application was granted.

Kahiya and Chimakure's arrest followed defamation charges levelled against editor Brezhnev Malaba and reporter Nduduzo Tshuma, of the provincial state-controlled daily *The Chronicle*, over an article exposing alleged police involvement in a maize scandal at the Grain Marketing Board (GMB), published in the paper in February.

According to Section 96 of the Criminal Law (Codification and Reform) Act 2004, a person commits an act of criminal defamation if he or she publishes a 'statement' which is 'false' and 'causes serious harm to the reputation' of a person. The offence is punishable with a fine and/or a prison term of up to two years. In such cases the state would need to prove that the accused had the intention to injure the reputation of another. The accused would have such intention if, in the words of the law, 'whatever his motives, he knows or at least foresees the possibility that what he is doing is to publish unlawful defamatory matter concerning the complainant.' Prosecutions under this section are 'rare'.[27]

4.5   Interception of Communications Act 2007

The Interception of Communications Act (ICA), dubbed the 'spying act', was signed into law in August 2007. It empowers the government to open private postal mail, eavesdrop on telephone conversations and intercept faxes and e-mails. The chief of defence intelligence, the director-general of the Central Intelligence Office (CIO), the commissioner of police, the commissioner general of the Zimbabwe Revenue Authority, or any of their nominees are authorised to request interception warrants from the minister of transport and communications without any mention of court permission being granted for such requests.[28]

---

27 Ibid.
28 Interception of Communications Act, Section 5(1).

According to Section 9 of the Act, internet service providers (ISPs) and telecommunications operators must install the necessary monitoring software themselves at their own cost to assist the government in its spying mission:

1) A service provider must ensure that –
    a) its postal or telecommunications systems are technically capable of supporting lawful interceptions at all times {...};
    b) it installs hardware and software facilities and devices to enable interception of communications at all times or when so required, as the case may be;
    c) its services are capable of rendering real time and full time monitoring facilities for the interception of communications;
    d) all call-related information is provided in real-time or as soon as possible upon call termination;
    e) it provides one or more interfaces from which the intercepted communication shall be transmitted to the monitoring centre;
    f) intercepted communications are transmitted to the monitoring centre via fixed or switched connections, as may be specified by the agency; [...]
2) A service provider who fails to give assistance in terms of this section shall be guilty of an offence and liable to a fine not exceeding level twelve or to imprisonment for a period not exceeding three years or to both such fine and such imprisonment.

Although the Zimbabwe Internet Service Providers Association (ZISPA) initially opposed the legislation, it put up no further resistance after its passing in parliament, saying it had no choice but to go along with the new requirements. 'We're putting in place measures to comply,' said Shadreck Nkala, ZISPA chairman and group executive for Telecontract, which owns Telconet, an ISP.[29]

4.6 Privileges and Immunities and Powers of Parliament Act (1991)

The intention of this Act is to punish any act of contempt of parliament. Section 10 makes it a criminal offence to publish defamatory statements about the conduct of members of parliament or in a parliamentary committee or which reflects negatively on the proceedings or character of parliament or a committee of parliament.

Section 22 makes it an offence to:

---

29 Interview with Shadreck Nkala, ZISPA chairman and group executive for Telecontract, 23 July 2008.

i) wilfully fail or refuse to obey an order of Parliament;

ii) refuse to be examined before or to answer any lawful and relevant questions put by Parliament or a committee of Parliament;

iii) publish the proceedings of a committee of Parliament or evidence given before such a committee has reported to Parliament;

iv) wilfully misrepresent any speech made by a member of Parliament;

v) wilfully publish a false or perverted report of any debate or proceedings or character of parliament or a committee of Parliament.

A fine or imprisonment or both can be ordered by parliament's privileges committee for contraventions of the Act. The decision of parliament can be placed before the High Court for review.

In 1992 the then editor of the *Financial Gazette*, Trevor Ncube, and a reporter, Regis Nyamakanga, appeared before the committee for alleging that government ministers and others had received favours from a corrupt businessman. They cited as their source an unnamed member of a parliamentary committee. The privileges committee ordered them to reveal the name of their source and threatened to jail them if they did not comply. They finally gave way to pressure.[30]

4.7 Access to information

Section 5 of the Access to Information and Protection of Privacy Act (AIPPA) establishes a general right to access information.

Persons requiring information from a public body are expected to put their request in writing and the institution has 30 days in which to reply. Only the heads of such public bodies are allowed to respond to requests for information. In the case of the police, only two officials are allowed to respond to the applicant – the police commissioner or the police spokesperson. They often refuse to provide information or are simply unavailable, particularly to journalists from the privately owned media.

Sections 14 to 25 deal with 'protected information', that is, categories of documents which are exempted from disclosure. This includes all cabinet documents, including draft legislation, advice or recommendations provided to public bodies (with some exceptions) and information whose disclosure would affect relations between different levels of government or may result in harm to the economic interest of a public body.

Of particular concern is Section 9(4)(c) which reads: 'The head of a public body may refuse a request for a record or part of a record if granting access to such a record is

---

30 T. Hondora, *Media Laws in Zimbabwe*, published by MISA and KAS in or about 2005, p. 125.

not in the public interest.' Such a catch-all provision could be used to refuse access to virtually all documents simply because the 'head of a public body' declares them to be not in the 'public interest'.

The provision does not comply with Clause IV(1) of the Declaration of Principles on Freedom of Expression in Africa which states: 'Public bodies hold information not for themselves but as custodians of the public good and everyone has a right to access this information, subject only to clearly defined rules established by law.'

5   The media and the inclusive government

The 'Global Political Agreement' between ZANU PF and the two MDC formations of September 2008 as well as the Constitutional Amendment (19) of February 2009 contain important provisions regarding the media.

Article 19 of the Agreement recognises 'the importance of freedom of expression and the role of the media in a multi-party democracy' and calls for 'the issuance of licences' to broadcasters other than the 'public broadcaster' (see chapter three). It also expresses the shared view that:

> ... the public and private media shall refrain from using abusive language that may incite hostility, political intolerance and ethnic hatred or that unfairly undermines political parties and other organisations. To this end, the inclusive government shall ensure that appropriate measures are taken to achieve this objective.

One such 'appropriate' measure is contained in Constitutional Amendment 19. Section 39 gives the Zimbabwe Media Commission created by AIPPA constitutional status. Like other commissions established by the basic law it is thus constitutionally protected against 'the direction or control of any person or authority' and required not to 'discriminate against, or favour unduly, any political party or group'. However, one clause in the new section inserted in the constitution to this effect paves the way for continued statutory interference in the freedom of the media:

> An Act of Parliament may confer powers on the Zimbabwe Media Commission, including power to ... take disciplinary action against journalists and other persons employed in the press, print or electronic media, or broadcasting who are found to have breached any law or any code of conduct applicable to them [new section 108C(4)(b].

rt Term Emergency Recovery Plan (STERP), which was presented by the vernment on 19 March 2009 and is meant to encourage the international nity to assist with the reconstruction of the country, in its Section 28 again ...ses the importance of creating a vibrant and free media as an important part of ...nocratising institutions. This entails liberalising the air waves, freeing the media, and ensuring that plural voices are heard through both electronic and print media.[31]

6 Conclusions and recommendations

Zimbabwe is about to undertake reforms in nearly all spheres of political and social life. This effort must be as inclusive and open as possible, and closely involving civil society at large from the very beginning.

A free media is the essential prerequisite for such a democratic reform process. Therefore, the entire regulatory framework for the media needs to be reconstituted, and a range of repressive laws that restrict freedom of the media and violate international standards should be amended or scrapped altogether.

The inclusive government instituted in February 2009 provides a possible opening for such a comprehensive overhaul.

Recommendations

Constitution

Section 20 of the present constitution does not sufficiently guarantee freedom of expression, including freedom of the media. The debate on a new section in this regard in a new constitution should be guided by the Declaration of Principles on Freedom of Expression in Africa of the African Commission on Human and Peoples' Rights (2002) which states:

> Freedom of expression and information, including the right to seek, receive and impart information and ideas, either orally, in writing or in print, in the form of art, or through any other form of communication, including across frontiers, is a fundamental and inalienable human right and an indispensable component of democracy.
>
> Everyone shall have an equal opportunity to exercise the right to freedom of expression and to access information without discrimination.

31 Short Term Emergency Recovery Plan (STERP), March 2009, accessed from allafrica.com/peaceafrica/resources/ view/00117757.pdf

Consideration should also be given to the 1996 Constitution of South Africa in it. Section 16 which provides a guarantee of freedom of expression seen as one of the most progressive and democratic worldwide:

> Everyone has the right to freedom of expression, which includes –
> - freedom of the press and other media;
> - freedom to receive or impart information or ideas;
> - freedom of artistic creativity; and
> - academic freedom and freedom of scientific research.
>
> The right (outlined above) does not extend to –
> - propaganda for war;
> - incitement of imminent violence; or
> - advocacy of hatred that is based on race, ethnicity, gender or religion, and that constitutes incitement to cause harm.

Media laws in general

- Laws inhibiting the free operations of the media must be repealed without delay. The most important of these is the Access to Information and Protection of Privacy Act (AIPPA).
- The provision in Constitutional Amendment 19 of February 2009 to set up a Zimbabwe Media Commission must be revisited. At the very least such a commission must not be allowed to interfere with the freedom and self-regulation of the media.
- The Public Order and Security Act (POSA) which, in conjunction with AIPPA, severely limits the right of the media to freedom of expression, must be repealed without delay.
- There is no need for general media-specific legislation (South Africa, for example, has no press law) or a specific registration law – publishing companies should be subject to the companies act like every other enterprise.
- All laws that might curtail or have an impact on freedom of expression (such as secrecy laws) need to be reviewed and – where necessary – amended. Consideration should be given to the introduction of a right to reply and the protection of sources.

Access to information

Currently, access by the public to information held by government authorities is regulated by the Access to Information and Protection of Privacy Act (AIPPA). This

Act needs to be replaced by a new access to information law. The guidelines set by the Declaration of Principles on Freedom of Expression in Africa provide a good model to be followed:

1) Public bodies hold information not for themselves but as custodians of the public good and everyone has a right to access this information, subject only to clearly defined rules established by law.

2) The right to information shall be guaranteed by law in accordance with the following principles:
    - everyone has the right to access information held by public bodies;
    - everyone has the right to access information held by private bodies which is necessary for the exercise or protection of any right;
    - any refusal to disclose information shall be subject to appeal to an independent body and/or the courts;
    - public bodies shall be required, even in the absence of a request, actively to publish important information of significant public interest;
    - no one shall be subject to any sanction for releasing in good faith information on wrongdoing, or that which would disclose a serious threat to health, safety or the environment save where the imposition of sanctions serves a legitimate interest and is necessary in a democratic society; and
    - secrecy laws shall be amended as necessary to comply with freedom of information principles.

3) Everyone has the right to access and update or otherwise correct their personal information, whether it is held by public or by private bodies.

The right of access to information should be guaranteed in the Constitution.

Voluntary Media Council of Zimbabwe
The Voluntary Media Council needs to be strengthened by:

- Ensuring that the Council represents all the media in the country and encouraging editors of state-controlled media to join the body;
- Embarking on a comprehensive public relations campaign to make readers, listeners and viewers of the media aware of the existence of a complaints body;
- Organising a series of workshops to train media practitioners in all media on professional standards of journalism as outlined in the code of ethics.

When the statutory media commission is established with the right to take disciplinary action against journalists, the media fraternity in Zimbabwe should follow their peers in other African countries such as Botswana, Uganda or Nigeria by not recognising this commission as a complaints body and offering the public their own effective Voluntary Media Council as an alternative.

3
The Broadcasting Landscape

1   The state broadcaster

The ZBC is exclusively owned by government. It operates one television channel and five radio stations: National FM broadcasting in 17 local languages; Power FM, a youth music station; Radio Zimbabwe broadcasting in Shona and Ndebele; English language Spot-FM and SW-24/7 transmitting on short and medium wave.

For more details see chapter six.

2   Commercial/private broadcasters

On 22 September 2000 the Supreme Court granted privately owned Capital Radio the right to broadcast, thus *de jure* ending the monopoly of the state broadcaster, although this decision did not translate into practice. The court ruled that the station had the right to import equipment and to operate a broadcasting service and that Section 27 of the Broadcasting Act, which provided for the state's monopoly of the airwaves, violated the rights of freedom of expression and the freedom to impart information as stipulated in Section 20 of the Constitution of Zimbabwe.[32]

The court also declared unconstitutional sections of the Radio Communication Services Act which prohibited ownership of transmitters by broadcasting operators and provided for the allocation of frequencies by the Post and Telecommunications Corporation.

---

32 *Capital Radio (Private) Limited vs Minister of Information,* Post and Telecommunications, SC 99/2000.

However, the court dismissed the radio station's petition to start operating within ten days after the court decision. Instead, it ruled that the station had to wait for the government to end its monopoly through a new broadcasting law.

When Capital Radio went on air six days later without waiting for the state to amend its laws, its equipment was seized by the police.

The government then moved quickly to fill the legal vacuum created by the Supreme Court ruling. A Broadcasting Services Bill was drafted and promulgated through the Presidential Powers (Temporary Measures) Act and became an Act of Parliament on 3 April 2001.

The Act set up the Broadcasting Authority of Zimbabwe (BAZ) as a statutory regulator and precluded anyone but the state from owning transmitters in the country. The responsibility for all broadcasting transmission was given to a state controlled company, TransMedia.

The Broadcasting Services Act made it almost impossible for private players to enter the broadcasting sector. Prospective broadcasters were frustrated in particular by Section 6 which gave the minister of information and publicity sweeping powers over licensing, to the extent that he became a licensing authority unto himself (see chapter five).

Although the BAZ had received seven applications by the beginning of 2002, including one for a community radio licence, two for local commercial licences and one for a national commercial free-to-air television licence, none of these were granted. This led to the conclusion that the Act was not intended to open up the airwaves but actually to achieve the opposite.

The organisers of Capital Radio eventually moved to London and started operating as Shortwave Radio Africa (SW Radio Africa), broadcasting into Zimbabwe from the British capital.

SW Radio Africa (SWRA) is one of the extra-territorial radio stations trying to fill the gap in the provision of independent radio voices since May 2007. The station broadcasts for two hours daily from 18h00 to 20h00 and transmits on two short wave frequencies (currently 4880 and 11745 kHz). Its broadcasts are also available through MP3 Podcasts and its news headlines are disseminated through SMS to approximately 30 000 subscribers three times a week. SWRA has Zimbabwean staff at its London offices and uses correspondents inside Zimbabwe.

Another external service is Studio 7 – a US-government funded radio programme produced by Voice of America. The station broadcasts on SW and AM bands from the US, via a repeater station in Botswana, for two hours every evening. The people involved with the project are mostly former Zimbabwean journalists forced into exile by the persecution from the Zimbabwean government after 1999.

Voice of the People (VoP) has been on air since mid-2000 and broadcasts from 06h00–07h00 every weekday morning in Shona, Ndebele and English on 11 610 KHZ. Its programmes include news bulletins and current affairs, as well as short segments on the economy, health (especially fighting the HIV/AIDS pandemic), gender issues and agriculture. In August 2002 VoP's offices in Harare were destroyed in a bomb blast set off by unknown assailants. Police are still to bring those responsible to book. In December 2005, VoP was closed down by the state after police raided its offices, seized its equipment and arrested three female journalists. VoP then relocated its production studios to South Africa. All material is sent via Internet to South Africa where the programme is put together, sent on to the Netherlands, again by Internet, and transmitted by Radio Netherlands via satellite to a transmitter in Madagascar, from where it is beamed back into Zimbabwe on short wave.

A fourth broadcaster producing programmes inside the country but also transmitting its signal into the country from abroad, is Zimbabwe Community Radio (see below).

All these stations take pride in the fact that they offer a range of voices, including individuals affiliated with ZANU PF as well as MDC representatives and supporters. But they acknowledge that their limited transmission time of only one or two hours a day is not enough to balance the messages carried for 24 hours a day on government stations.

Even though they are broadcasting on unattractive short wave frequencies, these stations are of great concern to ZANU PF. Before the March 2008 elections government installed equipment obtained from China to jam SW and AM broadcasts into the country.

ZANU PF also insisted that these stations be put on the agenda of negotiations with the Movement for Democratic Change (MDC), which led to the signing of the Global Political Agreement and the establishment of the inclusive government (see chapter two). In its Article 19, the document elaborates at length on the future of these broadcasting operators:

> **Recognising** the importance of the right to freedom of expression and the role of the media in a multi-party democracy.
>
> **Noting** that while the provisions of the Broadcasting Services Act permit the issuance of licences, no licences other than to the public broadcaster have been issued.
>
> **Aware** of the emergence of foreign-based radio stations broadcasting into Zimbabwe, some of which are funded by foreign governments.
>
> **Concerned** that the failure to issue licences under the Broadcasting Services Act to alternative broadcasters might have given rise to external radio stations broadcasting into Zimbabwe.

Further concerned that foreign government-funded external radio stations broadcasting into Zimbabwe are not in Zimbabwe's national interest.

Desirous of ensuring the opening up of the airwaves and ensuring the operation of as many media houses as possible.

19.1 The Parties hereby agree:-

a) that the government shall ensure the immediate processing by the appropriate authorities of all applications for re-registration and registration in terms of both the Broadcasting Services Act as well as the Access to Information and Protection of Privacy Act;

b) all Zimbabwean nationals including those currently working for or running external radio stations be encouraged to make applications for broadcasting licences, in Zimbabwe, in terms of the law;

c) that in recognition of the open media environment anticipated by this Agreement, the Parties hereby:-

i) call upon the governments that are hosting and/or funding external radio stations broadcasting into Zimbabwe to cease such hosting and funding;
and

ii) encourage the Zimbabweans running or working for external radio stations broadcasting into Zimbabwe to return to Zimbabwe ...

While the commitment to the 'opening up of airwaves' is commendable, the frequent and extensive reference made to 'foreign-based radio stations' is worrying. These stations were started – as the Agreement itself points out – precisely because of the 'failure to issue licences' under the Broadcasting Services Act. The fact that the opposition parties should have agreed to summarily declaring 'foreign government funded external radio stations broadcasting into Zimbabwe' to be 'not in Zimbabwe's national interest' is odd, given that these broadcasters helped to give them a voice on the airwaves and spread their message to the electorate when there was hardly any other platform for them to do so. Also, calling on 'governments that are hosting and/ or funding external radio stations ... to cease such hosting and funding' reveals a poor understanding of what the independent regulation and funding of broadcasting is all about. Most of the external stations are funded by non-governmental organisations, not by governments, and technical assistance is provided by radio stations licensed not by governments but by independent regulators. In any case, it is premature to demand the closure of such stations before non-state-controlled broadcasting is possible in Zimbabwe.

3 Community broadcasting

Although the Broadcasting Services Act of 2001 provides for community broadcasting, no community radio has been licensed yet.

To prepare themselves for the day when licences will actually be granted for community broadcasting, radio activists around the country have formed nine Community Radio Initiatives (CRIs), with another two in the pipeline. Together they have established the Zimbabwe Association of Community Radio Stations (ZACRAS) to lobby for their interests and seek technical assistance on behalf of their members.

One of these initiatives, Radio Dialogue[33] in Bulawayo, has developed innovative ways of reaching its audience over the past few years even before going on air. They have also assisted and inspired other CRIs, including Community Radio Harare (CORAH), to do the same. For example, they produce programmes and disseminate them on cassette tapes or compact discs which they hand out to drivers of minibuses who play them on their runs. These tapes and CD's are also distributed to the members of many community groups in their geographical areas.

In addition, Radio Dialogue and other CRIs carry out community meetings on matters that directly affect residents in the form of a simulated live broadcast, using this as an advocacy tactic to demonstrate the possibilities and benefits of community radio. As a result these communities are then more ready to support community radio campaigns and increase pressure on especially local and provincial MPs to lobby their parties and national government for the granting of independent community radio licences. All these CRIs, led by Radio Dialogue, also offer basic training in radio journalism and production skills, and some of them operate (or have access to) basic production studios and equipment.

Between 2007 and 2008, Radio Dialogue addressed various issues such as the mealie-meal (maize) shortages, the Zimbabwe Electricity Distribution Company (ZEDC) and its demand that each household install a metre box that would measure the amount of electricity consumed in each household, thefts in neighbourhoods, or the lack of refuse collection, among others.

The successes of such meetings include the reversal of ZEDC's planned introduction of metre boxes. Residents formed action groups against the plan, citing that they could not afford the boxes, drew up a petition and letters to relevant authorities, and set up committees to meet with their members of parliament. Generally, these meetings give the community of Bulawayo the opportunity to come face-to-face with representatives of the authorities, to get answers to questions they have and give their opinions as well.

---

33 www.radiodialogue.co.zw

Radio Dialogue records the proceedings on cassette or compact disc and strategically distributes them to the community – an alternative form of broadcasting.[34]

As a means to put pressure on the new government to live up to the commitment made in the Global Political Agreement to 'ensure the immediate processing by the appropriate authorities of all applications' for broadcasting, Radio Dialogue initiated a new 'foreign-based' radio station in April 2009. Zimbabwe Community Radio (ZCR) started broadcasting on short wave from the United Arab Emirates – with this introductory message: 'At present we are broadcasting from the United Arab Emirates. But we are happy to respond to the call in the political parties' agreement to return and broadcast in Zimbabwe. Just tell us when we will be welcome home.'[35] So far they have only managed to move a little closer to home: from September 2009 ZCR has been broadcasting from South Africa for an hour from 19h55 to 20h55 every day in English, Ndebele and Shona.

4   Technical standards and accessibility of services

4.1   Transmission infrastructure

Dating back to the colonial era, the transmitter system in Zimbabwe was basically designed to serve the urban areas where most white people lived.

Most parts of the country are therefore still not covered by television transmission because the network follows the country's urban road grid. The main transmitters are in Harare, with others located in the major cities and towns around the country. According to the principle director in the ministry of media, information and publicity there is between 20 and 25 per cent coverage for television transmission and 30 to 35 per cent for radio.[36]

According to the director of engineering and technical services at TransMedia – the government-owned sole signal transmission authority – transmitters along the transmission chain are still linked through telephone lines.[37] The use of optic fibre technology is still in its infancy. As a result television picture quality is extremely poor and grainy.

Failure to repair broken down equipment especially during the rainy season has resulted in the radius covered by some radio stations being reduced to as little as

---

34 Interview with Henry Masuku, Radio dialogue advocacy Officer, 22 April 2008.
35 Flyer issued by initiators of Zimbabwe Community Radio in February 2009.
36 ZACRAS, Government discuss community radio, ZBC Online News, 19 August. Retrieved at http://www.newsnet.
    co.zw/index.php?nID=16641, accessed 20 August 2009.
37 Interview with Hilda Mutseyekwa at TransMedia, 24 February 2008.

10 km, whereas the technology was initially designed to cover 100 km.

The transmission zone thus excludes most rural areas and small towns that struggle to get any video and audio feed – these areas remain 'dead zones'. Most people in the border areas have been forced to live without radio and television transmission either because of poor or extremely intermittent reception of ZBC stations or the absence of transmission centres in some of these areas. Many depend on foreign television and radio transmissions from neighbouring South Africa, Botswana and Mozambique.

The chief executive officer of TransMedia, Alfred Mandere, says: 'The country's radio and television transmitters are antiquated, as most of the equipment dates back to 1974. Nearly all our equipment is now beyond its useful lifespan and we are even surprised that broadcasters are still on air because the situation is really bad.'[38]

Mandere says the organisation does not have enough money to buy modern equipment and is actually in the process of appealing to government to help harness the needed foreign currency for the plan. The money would be used to purchase antenna systems and transmission equipment for both radio and television, and for the refurbishment of obsolete machinery. This plan has, however, been on the cards since 2006 and because of the economic difficulties that the country is facing, TransMedia has not been able to obtain any form of funding from the government.

TransMedia's financial position is worsened by the fact that it is unable to charge the ZBC commercial rates for their services. In order to generate revenue to sustain its operations, TransMedia has resorted to providing services like webcasting to other organisations in the country.

4.2 Access to electricity

Less than 50 per cent of all households have electricity.[39] Urban areas are better off in this regard. Out of all households with electricity, 80 per cent are in urban areas and only 15 per cent in rural areas.[40]

Batteries are thus the main means for the majority of rural households to power their television and radio sets. However, due to economic difficulties these have become increasingly unaffordable and unavailable.

Since 2006, Zimbabweans have been experiencing frequent power cuts, ranging from five to ten hours a day. The capacity of the country's aging power plants has been declining because there has been very little investment as Zimbabwe battles severe foreign currency shortages.

---

38 Interview with Alfred Mandere, chief executive officer of TransMedia, 28 March 2008.
39 Southern African Power Pool (SAPP), 2007.
40 Ibid.

4.3 Production equipment

Currently, the basic tool for collection of television news at ZBC is the Electronic News Gathering (ENG) camera and the digital audio recorder, with the broadcaster using mainly Digital Video Cassette (DVC)-Pro format. Television production uses state-of-the-art digital technology, installed in 2004 with the assistance of Iran, for post-production and studio-based work, with a fully equipped studio available for news and news-related productions. The pre-production process is now computerised for both audio and video.[41]

According to ZBC's (former) chief executive officer, Henry Muradzikwa,[42] the broadcaster is trying its best to adopt new technologies so as to remain competitive and relevant to the industry.

'We will adopt new technologies to keep in league with other broadcasters in the quest to meet customer requirements, tastes and expectations. One of the major projects that we are currently undertaking should see the complete digitalisation of the broadcasting technology for both pre- and post-production purposes,' Muradzikwa said.

Audiovisual material from outstations is brought to Harare through microwave links with feeding points at Bulawayo, Masvingo, Mutare, Gweru and Chinhoyi. Microwave capability is also available at Kariba, Victoria Falls and Marondera, but is not being used at the moment due to lack of equipment. Audio material is collected through audio recorders and over the telephone from bureau correspondents and news sources for broadcasts from headquarters in Harare.

At the Montrose Studios in Zimbabwe's second largest city, Bulawayo, the technical situation is slightly different to that in the capital. In general, Bulawayo, which is situated in the Matebeleland province, has been neglected in terms of development. The studios still operate semi-digitally, meaning that they only use digital equipment in the editing of programmes produced for the Harare studios. For all other programmes they still depend on analogue technology.

---

41 Interview with Moffat Phiri, regional engineer for the ZBC Matebeleland Province based at the Montrose Studios in Bulawayo, 21 April 2008.
42 Henry Muradzikwa has, since the interview in March 2008, been replaced by Happisson Muchechetere, a known ZANU PF sympathiser.

5   Conclusions and recommendations

Clause V(1) of the Declaration of Principles on Freedom of Expression in Africa says:

> States shall encourage a diverse, independent private broadcasting sector. A State monopoly over broadcasting is not compatible with the right to freedom of expression.

It is obvious that Zimbabwe is in breach of this principle. The same goes for the one expressed in Clause V(2)(4):

> ... community broadcasting shall be promoted given its potential to broaden access by poor and rural communities to the airwaves.

The following recommendations are made:

- The Broadcasting Authority of Zimbabwe (BAZ) should issue broadcasting licences to commercial and community broadcasters so that the three-tier broadcasting system envisaged in the Broadcasting Services Act is realised.
- The ZBC television transmission system needs an urgent overhaul. New transmission towers should be constructed in strategic places across the country so that the whole population can be served by the ZBC.
- The state-owned signal company, TransMedia, should be supervised by the Broadcasting Authority of Zimbabwe (once a new Broadcasting Services Act is in place). It should be restructured to enable it to deal effectively with transmission problems facing the national broadcaster and to meet the challenges posed by digitalisation.
- The Broadcasting Services Act must allow for more than one additional signal carrier company and for commercial/community broadcasting services to operate their own transmitter network if they wish.

4
Digitalisation and its Impact

1 Preparedness for switch-over to digitalisation

The Zimbabwe Broadcasting Corporation (ZBC) and the government have been working towards the digitalisation of broadcasting stations throughout the country by gradually replacing analogue with digital production equipment. However, this has been done outside a policy framework that would take into consideration the whole process of migration from analogue to digital.

The country faces two major challenges in this regard: lack of funds and lack of skills. At the ZBC's Montrose Studios in Bulawayo, for example, government seems to have suspended the digitalisation programme because of lack of funding to buy the necessary equipment and also due to a shortage of skilled manpower to operate the digital equipment. Over the past decade most of the technicians/engineers at ZBC have moved into neighbouring countries for better opportunities.

The ZBC Harare studios are the only ones to have completely digitalised production equipment which became operational in August 2005. The digitalisation project was financed through a government credit facility with Iran for 5 million Euros.

From all the evidence available it seems unlikely that Zimbabwe will achieve digital migration by the deadline of 2015 set by the International Telecommunication Union (ITU), given that the country would have to re-equip its entire terrestrial transmitter network and essential production facilities. There is also no policy in place to assist viewers with the necessary purchase of set-top boxes to enable them to receive digital signals.

2   Convergence

The government seems to have recognised the importance of new information and communication technology (ICT) and in 2005 adopted the ICT Policy Document. There has been deregulation of the telecommunications industry since 1998, resulting in the formation of three mobile companies: Econet Wireless, Telecel and NetOne, the latter being government-owned.

Lack of access to broadband internet connection due to a limited number of access points[43] is the main obstacle to the reception of interactive multimedia services and ultimately convergence. Other challenges the mobile providers are facing include network congestion, inadequate communication infrastructure, lack of finance, limited management capacity, inadequate national bandwidth and the low tariffs that are stipulated by the Post and Telecommunications Regulatory Authority of Zimbabwe (POTRAZ). All this has resulted in a lack of expansion for most of the network providers with a negative impact on the introduction of new services like Third Generation (3G) technology.

Since its establishment, POTRAZ has failed to come up with a clear policy framework to regulate the Voice over Internet Protocol (VoIP) which allows consumers to make telephone calls using a broadband internet connection instead of the regular analogue phone line. So far, internet providers in Zimbabwe have an IAP Class B licence only, which allows them to transmit data via the internet but not voice.

3   Conclusions and recommendations

The need to migrate from analogue to digital transmission and the convergence of technologies are realities that cannot be ignored. Currently, however, there is no clear policy on either. Steps need to be taken to:

- Speed up the digitalisation process through clear policy guidelines and provision of funding;
- Establish a Digital Migration Taskforce to draw up a Digital Broadcasting Migration Paper for Zimbabwe;
- Launch a consumer education and awareness campaign to educate the public on the digital migration process;
-

---

43   R. Ndlovu, *A comprehensive ICT guide for Zimbabwe*, March 2009, accessed from thezimbabwetimes.com/?p=13790

- Launch a Green/White Paper process to assess the implications of Zimbabwe adopting a law on the convergence of broadcasting and telecommunications and the pros and cons of a converged regulator;
- Ensure that TransMedia as the signal provider company produces a strategic plan and action plan on broadcasting digital migration.

5
Broadcasting Legislation and Regulation

Broadcasting in Zimbabwe is regulated by the Broadcasting Services Act (BSA) of 2001 and two subsequent Broadcasting Services Amendment Acts of 2003 and 2007. As a mass medium it also falls under the provisions of the Access to Information and Protection of Privacy Act (AIPPA) of 2002 and its amendments of 2003 and 2007, all of which are described in chapter three.

1   The Broadcasting Authority of Zimbabwe (BAZ)

The Broadcasting Services Act 2001 in its Section 3 establishes the Broadcasting Authority of Zimbabwe (BAZ) as the regulatory and licensing authority for the sector. According to the First Schedule of the Act, the Posts and Telecommunications Authority of Zimbabwe (POTRAZ) 'shall allocate all frequencies for the purposes of broadcasting services to the [Broadcasting] Authority for planning and licensing, and the [Broadcasting] Authority shall manage and allocate the frequencies for all broadcasting systems or services in Zimbabwe.' The BAZ has the responsibility 'to plan and advise on the allocation and distribution of the available frequency spectrum [...]' and 'to receive, evaluate and consider applications for the issue of any broadcasting licence or signal carrier licence.' The Amendment Act 2003 gives the BAZ (and not the minister in charge of broadcasting, as was the case under the principal 2001 Act) the power to determine who is to be issued a licence and when, to set the terms and conditions applicable in each individual case and to decide on the amendment, suspension and cancellation of licences.

The BAZ board consists of twelve members (Section 5 of the Amendment Act). Nine of these are appointed by the president after consultation with the minister in charge of broadcasting and parliament's Committee on Standing Rules and Orders. Board members have to fulfil the following requirements:

a) two shall be persons chosen for their experience or professional qualifications in the field of broadcasting technology and broadcasting content respectively; and

b) one shall be a Chief as defined in the Traditional Leaders Act [Chapter 29:17] and nominated by the Council of Chiefs referred to in that Act; and

c) one shall be a legal practitioner of not less than five years' standing registered in terms of the law in force relating to the registration of legal practitioners; and

d) one shall be a public accountant of not less than five years' standing registered in terms of the law in force relating to the registration of public accountants; and

e) one shall be a representative of churches or other religious bodies chosen from a list of nominees submitted by groups considered by the Minister to be representative of churches or other religious bodies; and

f) three other members.

While the president is obviously free to choose the last mentioned 'three other members' at his or her own discretion, a further three members are appointed by the president from a list of six nominees submitted by the parliamentary committee.

The nomination and appointment process is not subject to any public involvement or input. In effect the president has an almost free hand to appoint a board of his or her choice, given that the Act only requires consultation with the minister and the parliamentary committee but not their consent. In respect of the list of six names to be submitted by the committee, there is a further caveat: subsection 5 of the amended Section 4 states: 'If any council or group or the Committee on Standing Rules and Orders ... fails to or refuses to submit any nomination within thirty days of being requested to do so by the Minister in writing, the President may appoint any person to hold office as a member of the Board in all respects.'

The Third Schedule of the Act provides for disqualifications meant to avoid conflicts of interest: persons with a financial interest in broadcasting, members of parliament, or of two or more other statutory bodies are not allowed to be a member of the BAZ board.

On 30 September 2009, Media, Information and Publicity Minister Webster Shamu (ZANU PF) announced the appointment of a new BAZ board[44] to be chaired by Tatataona Mahoso, the head of the former Media and Information Commission who had ordered the closure of independent newspapers, among them *The Daily News*, in 2003. This appointment is seen as a clear signal that ZANU PF wants to block the entry of new players which it may regard as critical of the party. Another point of concern is that among the 12 members are a retired army colonel and a retired general.

The minister's deputy, Jameson Timba (MDC-T), said the appointments took him by surprise: 'Minister Shamu did not see the benefit of my wise council in this matter.'[45] Prime Minister Morgan Tsvangirai announced that the issue would be 'revisited' and that 'appointments of board members of BAZ are the business of the President and the Prime Minister.'[46] He did not mention the role of parliamentary committee provided for in the Act.

In June 2009, the inclusive government announced that a new Information and Communications Technology Bill was in the offing which would merge the BAZ and POTRAZ into a National Information and Communications Technology Authority of Zimbabwe. This new body would provide for the licensing and regulation of telecommunications, broadcasting and postal services.

2 Licence conditions

According to Section 7 of the BSA, the Broadcasting Authority is in charge of licensing commercial, community and subscription broadcasting services. The licensing of 'public broadcasters' is regulated by Section 37 which says that the Zimbabwe Broadcasting Corporation 'shall be deemed to be licensed to provide every class of broadcasting service that it provided immediately before the date of commencement of this Act,' which took effect in April 2001. The BAZ is also responsible for licensing roadcasting, railcasting and webcasting services. This provision extends its powers of control to include internet radio and television as well as pre-recorded programmes for reception by passengers on any public transport or railway service.

Section 10 of the BSA states that the BAZ will invite applications for licences through a notice in the *Government Gazette* and in a national newspaper. Since 2001, the BAZ has made two such calls for licence applications, neither of which resulted in the licensing of any new broadcaster.

---

44 *The Herald*, 1 October 2009.
45 *Zimbabwe Independent*, 2 October 2009.
46 *ZimOnline*, 7 October 2009, accessed from www.zimonline.co.za

The Act limits cross-ownership of broadcasting services and newspapers (Section 19). Among others, a licensee is not allowed to control more than one broadcasting service or simultaneously own a newspaper or more than 10 per cent of shares of a newspaper company.

The Act also does not allow any foreign ownership (Section 8) but this provision is qualified by Broadcasting Services Amendment Act, 2007. Section 7 – using a formulation lifted almost word for word from AIPPA – gives the minister in charge of broadcasting 'absolute discretion' to 'grant exemptions ... and permit the Authority to issue any broadcasting licence to an individual or body corporate approved by the Minister in which the controlling interest or any portion thereof is held by persons who are not citizens of Zimbabwe.'

All broadcasting licences are valid for ten years. They can be cancelled or suspended – after a public inquiry – if a broadcaster does not comply with any of the licence conditions.

Section 39 of the Broadcasting Services Act provides for basic 'public service obligations' for all broadcasting licensees. They have to provide 'sufficient coverage of national events' (without 'national events' being defined) and 'when providing an information service, provide a fair, balanced, accurate and complete service.'

These conditions apply to all three tiers of broadcasters – public, commercial and community. In addition, the 2007 Broadcasting Services Amendment Act introduced a Seventh Schedule to the principal act which outlines specific licence conditions applying to each of these categories in turn.

The requirements for 'the broadcasting service operated by a public broadcaster' are that it shall:

a) make programmes available to Zimbabweans in all the languages commonly used in Zimbabwe; and

b) reflect both the unity and diverse cultural and multilingual nature of Zimbabwe; and

c) strive to be of high quality in all the languages served; and

d) provide news and public affairs programming which meets the highest standards of journalism, and which is fair and unbiased and independent from government, commercial or other interests; and

e) include significant amounts of educational programming [...]; and

f) enrich the cultural heritage of Zimbabwe by providing support for traditional and contemporary artistic expression; and

g) strive to offer a broad range of services aimed in particular at children, women, the youth and the disabled; and

h) include programmes commissioned from independent producers; and

i) include programmes featuring national sports as well as developmental and minority sports.

The same schedule requires commercial broadcasters, 'when viewed collectively', to:

a) provide a diverse range of programmes addressing a wide section of the Zimbabwe public; and

b) make programmes available in all the languages commonly used in the areas which the broadcasters are licensed to serve; and

c) reflect the culture, character, needs and aspirations of the people in the regions which the broadcasters are licensed to serve; and

d) provide an appropriate but significant amount of Zimbabwean programming; and

e) regularly include news and information programmes, including discussion on matters of national and regional, and, where appropriate, local significance; and

f) meet the highest standards of journalism.

For community broadcasters the Act requires that they 'shall reflect the needs of the people in the community concerned, including their cultural, religious, language and demographic needs', and:

a) provide a distinct broadcasting service dealing specifically with community issues which are not normally dealt with by the public broadcasters or commercial broadcasters whose services cover the same area; and

b) be informational, educational and entertaining; and

c) concentrate on providing programmes that highlight community issues such as developmental issues, health care, basic information and general education, environmental affairs, and the promotion of local culture; and

d) promote a sense of common purpose within the community.

Section 24 of the Act gives the Broadcasting Authority the right to develop codes of conduct for broadcasters and to enforce such codes by imposing 'monetary and other penalties' in case of breaches. It does not provide any more details on sanctions and procedures.

Section 40 prescribes that 'every licensee shall establish a procedure for dealing with complaints by consumers of its services' which have to be attended to 'within 14 days'. If this deadline is not kept or the complainant is not satisfied with the remedy offered by the broadcasting station, he/she may turn to the Authority. The procedures for dealing with such complaints are not prescribed by law and have to be developed by the Authority.

The Sixth Schedule of the Broadcasting Services Act 2001 contains detailed quota on mandatory local content for all three tiers of broadcasting. A television broadcasting licensee has to ensure that 75 per cent of its programming content 'consists of local television content and material from Africa'. More specifically, 70 per cent of its drama, social documentary and 'knowledge-building' programming as well as 80 per cent of its current affairs, educational and children's programming 'must be of Zimbabwean origin'. Subscription television operators must broadcast at least 30 per cent local content. Music broadcast by radio stations – regardless of their programming format and character – has to be predominantly music produced in Zimbabwe (at least 75 per cent) and a further 10 per cent from Africa – leaving a balance of 15 per cent for music from outside the continent.

These requirements on local content have not been subject to any public debate or participation by stakeholders. While quota for local content are normal practice in most countries, the Zimbabwean conditions are excessive and unrealistic, especially in light of the small and struggling cultural production industry. Furthermore, the enforcement of such a high quota is bound to result in deliberately insulating Zimbabweans from information and culture originated outside the country and thus significantly reducing their knowledge of and exposure to the world.

3   Conclusions and recommendations

The regulatory mechanisms for broadcasting in Zimbabwe do not comply with major regional and international freedom of expression instruments. Clause 7 of the Declaration of Principles on Freedom of Expression in Africa states:

1) Any public authority that exercises powers in the areas of broadcast or telecommunications regulation should be independent and adequately protected against interference, particularly of a political or economic nature.

2) The appointments process for members of a regulatory body should be open and transparent, involve the participation of civil society, and shall not be controlled by any particular political party.

3) Any public authority that exercises powers in the areas of broadcast or telecommunications should be formally accountable to the public through a multi-party body.

In Zimbabwe, the Broadcasting Authority's board is appointed by the president without any involvement of civil society or meaningful participation of parliament. Therefore, the regulator has neither administrative, financial nor institutional independence.

The state broadcaster ZBC still retains its monopoly on broadcasting.

The 2001 Broadcasting Act and its two amendments appear to be putting up a mere façade. They create the illusion of a broadcasting authority tasked with regulating the sector at arms length from the government and licensing commercial and community broadcasters independently, while in effect power and control over broadcasting remain firmly in the hands of the president and the minister in charge of broadcasting.

Recommendations

- A policy on broadcasting legislation and regulation should be developed with input from all stakeholders and the public at large.
- On the basis of this policy, the Broadcasting Services Act should be reviewed in its entirety and replaced as a matter of urgency by a new broadcasting regulatory law with the aim of creating an independent broadcasting authority. This law must be drafted in accordance with regional and international freedom of expression instruments.
- Broadcasting and telecommunications regulation should remain separate so that an independent broadcasting regulator can focus on the development of a diverse, vibrant and sustainable broadcasting industry in the country.
- The constitution should establish an independent broadcasting regulator.
- The local content policy should be subjected to thorough debate throughout the country and the broadcasting regulator should call for position papers from interested stakeholders. Realistic and achievable local content quotas should then be set, which will not have the effect of insulating Zimbabwe from global news, views and knowledge.
- The public complaints system for broadcasting should be reviewed and established in accordance with Clause 9 of the Declaration of Principles on Freedom of Expression in Africa which states:

1) A public complaints system for print or broadcasting should be available in accordance with the following principles:
   a) complaints shall be determined in accordance with established rules and codes of conduct agreed between all stakeholders; and
   b) the complaints system shall be widely accessible.
2) Any regulatory body established to hear complaints about media content,

including media councils, shall be protected against political, economic or any other undue interference. Its powers shall be administrative in nature and it shall not seek to usurp the role of the courts.

3)   Effective self-regulation is the best system for promoting high standards in the media.

It is recommended therefore that the complaints system for broadcasting should be the responsibility of the Voluntary Media Council of Zimbabwe.

• Members of boards and staff of the new independent broadcasting regulator should be trained in issues of regulation, for example, convergence and implications on regulation, allocation of frequency spectrum as well as the licensing and monitoring of broadcasters' compliance with licence conditions.

6

The Zimbabwe Broadcasting Corporation

The Broadcasting Services Act 2001 in its Section 2 defines 'public broadcaster' as 'the Zimbabwe Broadcasting Corporation ... or any other broadcasting entity established by law which is wholly owned or controlled by the State'.

Sections 36 and 37 of the same act deal with the establishment and licensing of the 'public broadcaster'. With the creation of the Broadcasting Authority of Zimbabwe (BAZ) as the broadcasting regulatory and licensing authority, these provisions became necessary to ensure continued legal status for the ZBC and its uninterrupted functioning as the state broadcaster. Section 37 says that 'the Broadcasting Corporation shall be deemed to be licensed to provide every class of broadcasting service that it provided immediately before the date of commencement of this Act'.

1   Legislation

The Zimbabwe Broadcasting Corporation (Commercialisation) Act of 2001 repealed the original Zimbabwe Broadcasting Corporation Act of 1973. Under its Section 3 the ZBC was transformed into two successor companies: a broadcasting company which took over the functions of broadcasting and was to be known as Zimbabwe Broadcasting Holdings (ZBH), and a signal carrier company to take over the functions of signal carriage, TransMedia. Just a year later the Broadcasting Services Amendment Act 2002 in the section dealing with definitions reintroduced the name 'Zimbabwe Broadcasting Corporation' for the 'national broadcasting service formed as the successor to the former Corporation in terms of section 3 of the [Commercialisation Act]'.

According to the ZBC (Commercialisation) Act, the state is the only shareholder in both companies, holding its shares through nominees who 'shall be persons nominated by the Minister, after consultation with the President and in accordance with any directions that the President may give him [sic] and shall hold their shares on behalf of the state'.

Section 5 provides that 'any person so appointed to hold shares, shall do so nominally as an agent for the State'. And Section 3 gives both companies a clear mandate: 'In the performance of their functions, the successor companies shall give priority to serving the needs of the state, to the extent that it is compatible with sound business practice to do so.'

Thus, the national – and only – broadcaster in Zimbabwe is both state-owned and state-controlled, serving the state's interests.

Under Section 8, the board of governors is appointed by the minister of information and publicity in consultation with the president. There is no process of public nomination or any form of public involvement in the selection of the board. On 30 September 2009, Minister of Media, Information and Publicity Webster Shamu (ZANU PF), appointed a new ZBC board with Cuthbert Dube, the former manager of the Public Service Medical Aid Association (PSMAS) as chair and Doreen Sibanda, national executive director of the National Arts Gallery and wife of Misheck Sibanda, principal secretary to the president and the cabinet, as deputy chairperson. Other members include three retired army generals, two former ZBC employees, a musician, a bishop and a lawyer. The spokesman for the MDC-T coalition partner in government, Nelson Chamisa, said: 'The people were fished from ZANU PF rivers and ponds when there are other rivers. These characters have been appointed on a ZANU PF card.[47]

Political interference in the running of the affairs of the state broadcaster and the dismissal of top management have been frequent occurrences. Over a period of eight years the ZBC has gone through five chief executive officers. In the aftermath of the election on 29 March 2008, for example, in which Robert Mugabe as the presidential candidate of the ruling party was defeated, the ZANU PF government removed a number of senior managers of the ZBC, accusing them of not handling the election in a proper manner. The then CEO, Henry Muradzikwa, was fired by the board chairman, Justin Mutasa, as a result of pressure from the permanent secretary in the ministry of information and publicity, George Charamba.[48] Eight senior journalists and producers were also suspended soon afterwards amid accusations

---

47 *Zimbabwe Independent*, 2 October 2009.
48 'Muradzikwa accused of promoting opposition', *The Zimbabwe Times*, www.thezimbabwetimes.com/?p=141, accessed on 15 July 2008, and 'Head of State broadcaster fired for defying political orders', MISA-Zimbabwe www.ifex.org/en/content/view/full/93839

that they were sympathetic to the rival (and election winner) Movement for Democratic Change (MDC).[49]

Editorial independence at the ZBC is non-existent and the broadcaster is *de facto* run from the ministry. There are allegations of direct political interference which has resulted in news blackouts and stoppage of programmes which are deemed unsuitable by the state. At times, insiders say, the minister and the permanent secretary do not even have to give instructions for the banning of certain information, with the journalists resorting to self-censorship and 'sunshine journalism' out of fear of offending the 'big bosses'.[50]

2 Services of the Zimbabwe Broadcasting Corporation

The ZBC has one television channel operated by two departments – ZTV and Newsnet. The latter runs the news and current affairs programmes while the former takes care of all other programming. Newsnet is a private limited company and a subsidiary of the ZBC. It was registered as a private company with limited liability in terms of the Companies Act on 20 February 2004.

ZBC runs five radio stations:

- National FM is based in the capital Harare. It broadcasts 24 hours a day in 17 local languages and mainly focuses on news, music and socio-cultural content.
- Power FM is a 24-hour music station based in the Midlands capital Gweru. It targets the 15 to 30-year age group and is the purveyor of youth pop culture. Because of the lack of transmission equipment its programmes are fed through telephone lines to the main broadcasting station in Harare. This, of course, greatly affects the quality of sound that is finally relayed to the audience. At times, when the telephone lines are down, the station goes off air completely.
- Radio Zimbabwe is a full-spectrum station which broadcasts 24 hours a day in Shona and Ndebele from one of Harare's oldest suburbs, Mbare. Its programmes usually appeal to both rural and urban listeners.
- Spot-FM broadcasts in English. It is basically a news station that focuses on current affairs and debates. However, politics and economic issues generally

---

49 'Zimbabwe: ZBC Dismisses Eight Journalists', *allafrica*, 5 June 2008. Found at http://allafrica.com/stories/200806061017.html, accessed 6 November 2008.
50 Comment made by journalists during interviews about operations at the ZBC.

are avoided for fear of infringing the interests of the state. The station was originally based in Bulawayo, the second largest city, but has now moved to Harare.

- SW-24.7 was established in 2006 to counter extra-territorial 'pirate' radio stations broadcasting on SW and MW from outside the borders of Zimbabwe. The station is based in Gweru and was not on air at the time of writing.

3   Organisational structures of the ZBC

Jonathan Moyo, who was in charge of the ZBC from 2000 to 2005 as minister of information and publicity, acknowledged in an interview in 2008: '… we all know that broadcasting in Zimbabwe is considered a security area and is controlled by the State through the government.'[51] This principle is reflected in the lines of command within the corporation.

3.1   Lines of command

In theory, the chief executive officer runs the day-to-day activities at the broadcaster and on paper he or she is supposed to report to the board of governors. However, the practice has been for the ministry of information and publicity to make the final decisions on management and administrative issues. A case in point was the decision taken by the permanent secretary in the run-up to the elections in March 2008 to ban the flighting of advertisements from opposition parties without consulting the administration at the ZBC.[52]

However, there are some decisions such as those on editorial content regarding less sensitive issues that the CEO makes on his own in consultation with the management team and the board.

Reporting to the CEO – on a weekly basis – are the heads of the different departments: television, radio, news and current affairs, advertising and marketing, administration and finance, human resources and corporate affairs, engineering and technical services. Appointment to these positions is made by the CEO in consultation with the board of governors and the minister. Appointments are politically motivated and appointees are meant to fulfill the demands of government. This makes it very difficult for the CEO to discipline or fire these heads.

---

51 Interview with Jonathan Moyo on newzimbabwe.com on 12 January 2008, http://www.newzimbabwe.com/pages/zbc28.14316.html, accessed on 15 March 2009.
52 ZBC source who does not want to be named.

The next level in the hierarchy is that of managers. These are also political appointees and wield a lot of power over employees especially in the news department. There, a reference structure is in place from the heads of news to assignment editors, senior reporters, down to chief provincial reporters and reporters (with all higher positions traditionally held by ZANU PF members or sympathisers). 'Sensitive' or 'controversial' news stories are vetted by the heads of news. The day-to-day final compilation of television and radio news bulletins is supervised by the heads and at times requires clearing by the CEO and the ministry.

During interviews with journalists and other practitioners at the ZBC[53] the majority pointed out that there is a great deal of interference by ZANU PF officials which hinders the professional and efficient operations of the ZBC. Politicians often give instructions to managerial staff on their editorial preferences. It is also alleged that the divisions and factionalism within the party play out in the newsrooms. For instance, one journalist spoke of how a minister may phone in and give a directive regarding a story and soon after a permanent secretary will call and give instructions that counteract the initial directive. Politicians will stipulate who to report on and who not to report on.

Some of the journalists interviewed felt that the broadcaster was being used as a personal empire by those at the ministry of information and publicity, especially by the permanent secretary, George Charamba. One journalist who refused to be named said that Charamba was running the corporation as his personal fiefdom and this was demoralising to most of the staff as they felt that the core business of the broadcaster was no longer taking precedence. Charamba wields enormous power here, is untouchable, and staff at the broadcaster, including the ZBC board, is terrified of him,' said another journalist. All this has made journalists believe that whatever they do they have to be answerable to the government or individuals in the ministry rather than the general public.

One senior journalist concluded by saying that no matter how much they want to act professionally, they have no choice but to succumb to these pressures. 'People who love radio or television work have no other option but to join the state broadcaster, as there are no other players in the field.'

3.2 Editorial decisions versus advertising interests

Pressures on editorial decisions are also created by the ZBC's dependence on commercial income through advertisements and sponsorships (see chapter seven).

---

53 Thirty interviews conducted with ZBC staff in April 2008, July 2008 and July 2009.

Although the advertising and marketing management and that of editorial and programming departments are clearly separated, the sorry state of finances at the corporation sometimes forces the editorial management to follow the demands from advertisers as imposed by the marketing division.

The advertising and marketing department at the ZBC confirmed that they have been compelled to create programming environments in tune with what advertisers want. In addition, the final decision on advertising content rests with the CEO, and if he feels that some adverts are controversial he has to seek the approval of the minister.

3.3 Staffing and remuneration

As of July 2009 the ZBC employed a total of 196 people in programme production (reporters, producers, presenters) and 16 people in programme administration. The broadcaster was operating at 40 per cent capacity, due to serious staff shortages.

In late 2008, the Reserve Bank of Zimbabwe introduced a partial dollarisation of the economy and the 2009 first quarter budget was the first to be presented in US dollars. ZBC staff – like all other civil servants – are now paid in US dollars. According to records of the Zimbabwe Union of Journalists[54] junior reporters earned US$ 331 in September 2009, senior reporters US$ 370 and editors US$ 400, while top managers took home US$ 2 000 per month.

Print media reporters, by comparison, are better paid than their ZBC counterparts.[55] The ZBC is hamstrung in this regard because salaries at parastatals are set by the state. The problem is exacerbated by the perilous state of the economy and the lack of competition in the sector. Employment opportunities are extremely scarce and broadcast journalists have little choice but to cling to their jobs.

Lack of job security, poor salaries and poor working conditions have gravely affected the operations of the ZBC and the morale of staff. According to one journalist, if she was to get work outside the state broadcaster, she 'would take it without hesitation as there are better salaries, better chances of getting promoted and better recognition in the private sector.'

Over the years most of the experienced journalists have left the broadcaster for more lucrative jobs, either overseas or in the country. Some of the best reporters at ZBC are now reporting for foreign organisations like the South African Broadcasting Corporation (SABC), Reuters, BBC and Al-Jazeera, among others.

The current crop of editors and managers at the broadcaster have little experience

---

54 E-mail from the Zimbabwe Union of Journalists, 14 September 2009.
55 It is difficult to get official figures because most journalists are very secretive about their salaries.

7
Funding of the Zimbabwe Broadcasting Corporation

The national broadcaster, both under colonial rule and since independence, has been funded through public grants or subsidies, licence fees, and commercial advertising and sponsorship. Direct government grants have always been the predominant source of funding.

Between 1995 and 2000, resulting from a failed economic structural adjustment programme, advertising revenue and licence fees declined sharply. This left the ZBC in a serious financial crisis. To turn around the fortunes of the organisation, then Minister of Information and Publicity Jonathan Moyo initiated the process of commercialising the ZBC.

1   The ZBC commercialisation process

In 2002 the government decided to commercialise the state broadcaster so that it would be able to generate revenue independently from the treasury. The commercialisation process involved the redefinition of the vision, mission and core values of the ZBC and a staff cutting exercise that saw 60 per cent of the workforce retrenched. These processes were supported by the Zimbabwe Broadcasting (Commercialisation) Act, promulgated in 2001.

The Act split the ZBC into two independent holdings: the Zimbabwe Broadcasting Holdings (ZBH), being primarily responsible for the provision of broadcasting services, and TransMedia, a signal carrier company whose primary function is to provide signal transmission services in the country.

The broadcaster was further divided into nine Strategic Business Units (SBUs) with ZTV, the four radio stations, Newsnet, On-Air Systems (an engineering and technology unit), Channel C and National Television (NTV) constituting separate business units under one holding company. Each unit was headed by a chief executive officer (CEO).

Two of these business units – National Television (NTV) and Channel C – never took off. NTV was to have been a 24-hour full-spectrum television station broadcasting in Zimbabwe's 14 indigenous languages other than Shona and Ndebele and based in Bulawayo. Channel C was planned to be a joint venture with Multichoice Zimbabwe to start a 24-hour all-entertainment channel via satellite.

Only seven companies were actually set up and became operational. Under the new arrangement, all subsidiaries were required to fend for themselves, pay salaries to their staff, meet all operational costs and charge commercial rates for all their services. However, revenue flow was very erratic mostly due to the economic recession that the country was incrementally facing and the political interference that affected business management at the broadcaster.

For these reasons, coupled with mismanagement of the different business units, undercapitalisation and political interference, the business units failed to achieve any success.[57] In 2006 the government disbanded them and reverted back to the old system that had existed prior to the unbundling exercise. The realignment was meant, according to then Minister of Information Tichaona Jokonya, to restructure the broadcaster into a leaner and more viable entity.

In April 2004 the government agreed to write off a debt of more than Z$25 billion which the ZBC had amassed[58] and passed the Zimbabwe Broadcasting Debt Assumptions Act. A parliamentary report on the state of the broadcaster in the same year indicated that its finances were in a mess mainly because licence fee revenue had fallen over the previous ten years from 20 to 12 per cent of income in 2004.[59]

Poor debt collection mechanisms also worsened the corporation's financial woes. In particular it failed to recover substantial amounts of money from advertising agencies and direct clients.[60]

The situation was further exacerbated by the bloated workforce. Before retrenchments started in 2003, the ZBC's salary bill was way above its income. Most of this money went towards paying heads of departments and managers and not towards programming.[61]

57 *Parliamentary Report on Transport and Communications*, 31 May 2006.
58 Already in 2002, Mr. Munyaradzi Hwengwere, the then ZBC Chief Executive Officer, pointed out that liquidation was imminent as was evidenced by daily notices of attachment on property at the institution.
59 Parliament of Zimbabwe, *Second Report of the Portfolio Committee on Transport and Communications on Zimbabwe Broadcasting Holdings (ZBH)*, Fourth Session, Fifth Parliament. Harare, 2004, p. 21.
60 Interview with the Finance, Marketing and Advertising Department at ZBC, 24 June 2008.
61 *Parliamentary Report on Transport and Communications*, op.cit.

The corporation was dogged by a combination of high operating costs, lack of vestment in research and development, monotonous programme repeats resulting ,1 reduced audience figures, poor information management systems and costing policies, lack of strategic partners and limited sources of funding.[62]

2 Current sources of funding

The ZBC has not published an annual report since 1994. Therefore, details of its sources of funding were not available for this report.

On paper the major sources of funding are a mix of advertising and sponsorship, government grants, licence fees and the leasing of production facilities to other broadcasters.[63] However, the broadcaster is said to have received no grants from government since the promulgation of the ZBC Commercialisation Act in 2001.

Section 38 of the ZBC Commercialisation Act provides for licence fees payable to the ZBC by listeners and viewers. Such licence fees are to be paid at post offices or directly at ZBC premises and will form part of the funds of the company (sub-sections [a] and [b]). In Sections 38(c) and (d) of the act provision is made for inspections *in loco* to check for possession of television and/or radio sets and proof of payment of licence fees. The ZBC deploys its inspectors in the different suburbs and towns and these missions are usually announced by the national broadcaster in advance. The sub-sections also give police officers (or appointed inspectors) power to supervise the collection of licence fees, as they have the right to enter private homes or business premises to request proof of payment of licence fees.

The licence fee structure is determined by parliament. The process of setting the amounts payable and making them legally binding by gazetting them is usually time consuming and involves a lot of red tape. Given the hyperinflationary conditions obtaining until the new inclusive government took over, any amount or increase thus determined would have been eroded and rendered meaningless by the time it came into effect.

In December 2006, in contravention of the ZBC Commercialisation Act, the ZBC increased its licence fees. The new fees were promulgated by a statutory instrument published in the *Government Gazette* on 24 January 2007. In February 2007 the parliamentary Portfolio Committee on Transport and Communication questioned the ZBC's top management over the increase and hit out at the new amounts set, which they said were more than what the average worker earned in a month. Radio licence

62 Ibid.
63 Finance, Marketing and Advertising Dept, interview, op.cit.

fees at the time, for example, were pegged at Zim$150 000 when an average civil servant was earning less than Zim$117 000 a month.

The members of the committee also argued that proper procedures had not been followed because the ZBC did not have the legal right to determine licence fees and the committee ruled that the new fees were null and void.[64]

In March 2009, the ZBC with the approval of the ministry of information and publicity released a notice in terms of section 38(b) of the ZBC Commercialisation Act, setting the annual licence fees for the ZBC in US dollars and South African rands as follows:[65]

a)   Radio – rural, US$10 (ZAR100)
b)   Radio – urban US$20 (ZAR200)
c)   Television US$50 (ZAR500)
d)   Radio – business premises, US$50 (ZAR500)
e)   Television – business premises, US$100 (ZAR1 000)
f)   Radio – private vehicle, US$30 (ZAR300)
g)   Radio – employer-owned vehicle, US$80 (ZAR800)
h)   Radio and television – vehicle, US$100 (ZAR1 000).

Persons living in areas where there is no reception of ZBC signals still have to pay the fee. Critics[66] say that the amounts were neither based on an assessment of the ZBC's financial needs nor reasonable on social or economic grounds. For example, businesses running a fleet of vehicles (taxis or transport companies) would be charged inordinate amounts because they would have to pay for every single car radio.

The ZBC has been failing to collect enough licence fees to cater for its financial needs since 1980[67] and the current economic crisis has further worsened this situation. The number of licence holders from whom fees were collected has declined from 200 560 in 2002 to 146 000 in 2006, a reduction of 27.2 per cent.

ZBC Licensing Manager Stewart Luwizhi points out that resistance on the part of the public towards paying their licences is quite pervasive.[68] 'Most people have refused to open their doors to our inspectors,' said Luwizhi. 'The inspectors have stopped visiting the low-density suburbs where the "rich" are because the majority of them subscribe to satellite television. The collection process seems to gobble up a lot of the revenue that is collected because the licence fees are so low.'

---

64 Interview with Henry Muradzikwa, 22 March 2008. Further details accessed from 'Ignore Charamba, ZBC told' in *The Financial Gazette*, cited on http://www.zimbabwesituation.com/feb16_2007.html#Z2, accessed 25 March 2008
65 http://www.hararetribune.com/world/media/359-new-zbc-listener-license-fees-a-cause-for-concern.html, accessed 12 March 2009.
66 ZBC insiders who do not want to be named.
67 Interview with ZBC Licensing Manager Stewart Luwizhi, 5 March 2008.
68 Ibid.

According to Luwizhi there are a number of reasons why income from licence fees has gone down. These include the failure of government to produce a law to deal with defaulters, weaknesses in the collection system, resistance from viewers due to poor programming, especially after the local content quota stipulated by the Broadcasting Services Act and continuous interference by the government in programming.

With no increase in government funding forthcoming to make up for the shortfall, the ZBC at times resorted to unusual measures. At some point in 2004, for example, it ventured into horticulture at its premises in the Harare suburb of Highlands to augment revenue. With a lot of arable land available management went into partnership with the Chinese government growing tobacco and flowers. The money-making attempt was abandoned at the end of 2005, when the Chinese government pulled out.

For all these reasons, the ZBC's funding base, although at first glance apparently diversified, is in reality now largely dependent on advertising. From 2006 the share of advertising and sponsorship has risen to about half of total revenue.[69] Sources at the ZBC's marketing department said that due to its financial problems the broadcaster is now compelled to create a programming environment that is in tune with advertisers' preferences. This is particularly true when it comes to popular programmes such as the English Premier Soccer League and wrestling.

Long advertising breaks are the norm during sporting programmes and other popular programmes like the soap opera *Studio 263*.[70] The same trend is also apparent during news bulletins on both radio and television. 'We need to bring in money for the broadcaster to survive in these difficult times,' said one of the marketing managers.

Generally poor quality programming has inevitably led to most advertisers shying away from the ZBC and most viewers turning to satellite (free-to-air) broadcasting, starving the corporation of much needed revenue.

3 Spending

Details about spending were not made available to the researcher. ZBC employees feared that they might divulge information which is regarded as 'politically sensitive'. The fact that the ZBC has not published annual reports since 1994 suggests that there are discrepancies in the corporation's finances which the authorities do not want the public to know about.

---

69 Ibid.
70 This was the first ZBC 'soap opera' introduced in 2002 and has been very popular not only in Zimbabwe, but also in other African countries such as Malawi, Uganda and Zambia.

4   Conclusions and recommendations

The ZBC relies on three main sources of funding (government grants, licence fees, advertising), all of which are currently under threat. Due to the economic meltdown in the country, the government has drastically reduced its grants and the collection of licence fees has become unsustainable. This has resulted in poor programming leading to advertisers pulling out of the state broadcaster, thus leaving it in a financial quandary.

The basic precondition for any successful reform of funding is the passing and implementation of a new ZBC Act, that is, the transformation of the state into a credible public broadcaster offering quality programming designed to meet diverse audience needs.

In view of the present financial status of the ZBC it is recommended that:

- The new board commission a thorough audit of the corporation's financial status by an independent accounting firm;
- On the basis of a new programme policy the organisational structure of the ZBC be reviewed and reformed, in particular regarding administrative processes and expenses;
- On the basis of the new programme policy and organisational structure, a business plan be developed which reflects the financial needs of the ZBC and potential sources of revenue.

Regarding licence fees it is recommended that:

- Licence fees form the backbone of the ZBC's revenue sources because they provide stable, predictable multi-year funding and allow the broadcaster to plan and implement the necessary investment in programming and operational improvements;
- The amount of licence fees be fair and socially/economically justifiable;
- Households in regions not covered by ZBC signals not be required to pay licence fees;
- Efforts be made to improve significantly the compliance rate for payment of the fee among viewers and listeners.

In regard to revenues from the state fiscus, it is recommended that:

- An independent panel of experts determine the amount of subsidies needed by the ZBC over a three-year period to fulfill its public broadcasting mandate;

- Parliament fund the public broadcaster directly (and not through a ministry or department) on the basis of the amount determined by the panel of experts.

Concerning advertisements and sponsorships it is recommended that:

- The ZBC develop clear and strict guidelines on soliciting advertisements and conditions for accepting advertisements and programme sponsorships that will safeguard the broadcaster's editorial independence and clearly separate the responsibilities of editorial and marketing departments;
- The new broadcasting regulator embark on a process of public consultation with the objective to set appropriate limits to advertising and sponsorship on the ZBC.

8
Programming

1 Background

Programming at the ZBC needs to be understood and contextualised within the complex political and economic crisis that engulfed the country from 2000 onwards.

The vote against a proposed new constitution in the referendum held in February that year served as the first clear warning sign for the ruling party that its hitherto unquestioned dominance and presumed unassailability was coming under threat. This was followed two years later by general elections in which, for the first time since independence, a new political party (the Movement for Democratic Change, MDC) gained 57 out of 120 seats in parliament and the opposition candidate (Morgan Tsvangirai) nearly won the highly contested presidential vote.

The ruling ZANU PF party and government made the issue of land and its restitution to its original black Zimbabwean owners by virtually any means the central plank of their efforts to shore up support among the electorate. The state broadcaster was increasingly and more and more openly used to propagate this line as well as a whole new discourse of national/cultural identity, invocation of sovereignty and the pan-Africanist ideology that underpinned it.

With the coming into cabinet of Professor Jonathan Moyo as the new minister of information and publicity in 2000, programming of the ZBC went through fundamental changes.

The ZBC adopted a new mission statement, promising 'to provide world class quality programmes and services that reflect, develop, foster and respect the Zimbabwean national identity, character, cultural diversity, national aspirations and Zimbabwean and pan-African values.' It also introduced a new programming structure reflecting local content quota required under the Broadcasting Services Act (BSA) 2001. The law states in its Sixth Schedule that a television broadcasting licensee, that is, ZBC Television, must ensure that at least:

- 70 per cent of its drama programming consists of Zimbabwean drama;
- 80 per cent of its current affairs programmes consists of Zimbabwean current affairs;
- 70 per cent of its social documentary programming consists of Zimbabwean social documentary programming;
- 70 per cent of its knowledge-building programming consists of Zimbabwean informal knowledge-building programming;
- 80 per cent of its educational programming consists of Zimbabwean educational programming; and
- 80 per cent of its children's programming consists of Zimbabwean educational programming.

For radio, the Act requires that at least 75 per cent of the music broadcast must be Zimbabwean and another 10 per cent from other parts of Africa – leaving only 15 per cent for music from elsewhere in the world.

The government, through the department of information and publicity, used the local content provisions to introduce programmes mainly supportive of ZANU PF. Many programmes emanating from outside Zimbabwe were taken off the air. In their place, documentaries about the 1970s liberation war and programmes on land reform such as *Nhaka Yedu* (Our Heritage), *National Ethos* and the *New Farmer/ Murimi Wanhasi/Umlime Walamuhla* were introduced and given more and more prominence. All of them focused on issues of land and national identity – ZANU PF's campaign themes in the presidential and parliamentary elections in 2002 and 2005. These themes ran across all programming formats and genres (for example, children, education, current affairs and gender).

The 'national identity' project of the ZBC was a politically driven effort by the ruling party in complete disregard of the diverse opinions that Zimbabweans hold. The redefinition of Zimbabwean national identity and what it means to be Zimbabwean was narrow and those who did not agree with ZANU PF's philosophy were labelled as the 'other', 'evil'[71] or as 'sell-outs' representing the interests of the West. Thus, those working in civil society organisations, political opposition parties (in particular the MDC) and white Zimbabweans were either vilified by the state broadcaster or excluded from the airwaves altogether.

Music also featured prominently to promote the ruling party's policies. Protest songs from the country's well known artists like Oliver Mtukudzi, Thomas Mapfumo, Lovemore Majaivana, Albert Nyathi and others that had human rights, corruption and abuse of power as their main themes, were blacklisted and replaced with pro-government songs that were supportive of ZANU PF and the land reform programme and critical of Western leaders, especially then UK Prime Minister Tony Blair and then US President George W. Bush.

The government, through the office of the minister of information and publicity, Professor Jonathan Moyo, commissioned pro-ZANU PF music albums and jingles that filled the airwaves, leading to a total blackout of other types of music. Moyo himself, using public funds, promoted the production of a series of albums under the label 'Pax Afro', intended to 'communicate the regime's political messages of a resurrected liberation struggle, ultra-patriotism, land reclamation, anti-colonialism and pan-Africanism.'[72] The most prominent of these productions was the 26-track double CD titled *Back2Black*.

A study conducted by the Media Monitoring Project of Zimbabwe (MMPZ) in 2003 showed that one of the propaganda jingles, *'Rambai Makashinga'* (Continue Persevering), was being played on average 288 times a day on ZBC's four radio stations, which amounts to 8 640 times per month. On television, the jingle was flighted approximately 72 times a day, which amounts to 2 160 times a month.[73]

After the 2005 parliamentary elections, a new minister of information and publicity, Tichaona Jokonya, was appointed. Programming changed slightly, with some more diversity and foreign material being re-introduced – mostly old Hollywood productions and Nigerian films in the case of television. With regard to news and current affairs content, opposition parties, civil society organisations and other non-state actors were still locked out of the main programming and largely remained so up to the time of writing.

It needs to be borne in mind that many Zimbabweans, especially the large rural population, do not have or cannot afford access to any other media and rely almost

---

71 http://www.newzimbabwe.com/pages/electoral269.18288.html; Mugabe is quoted as saying 'The MDC opposition, formed at the behest of Britain in 1999, is on an evil crusade of dividing our people on political lines as they continue to fan and sponsor heinous acts of political violence targeting innocent citizens.'
72 D. Thram, Zvakwana-Enough, 'Media Control and Unofficial Censorship of Music in Zimbabwe', in: M. Drewett and M. Cloonan (eds), *Popular Music Censorship in Africa*, Ashgate Publishing, 2006.
73 M. Sibanda, 'Complete Control: Music and Propaganda in Zimbabwe', in: *Freedom of Musical Expression*, 2004. Downloaded at http://freemuse.inforce.dk/sw7086.asp, accessed 21 May 2008.

exclusively on ZBC radio for all their information needs. The kind of programming offered by the state broadcaster over the past few years has resulted in starving them of meaningful information and giving them a seriously skewed view of reality in the country and abroad.

Only a small minority of viewers were able to turn to free-to-air satellite television featuring South African TV channels. An important development in this regard was the 'discovery' of satellite TV decoders, known as WizTech, sourced from China and Dubai. They enable Zimbabweans to access encrypted South African channels such as SABC 1, 2 and 3 as well as e.tv without having to pay subscription fees.

2   Current programming of the ZBC

Other than the mission statement quoted above which speaks in general terms about what the broadcaster seeks to offer, the ZBC does not have a charter which would spell out its editorial policies, mandate and operational and programming guidelines.

Newsnet Pvt Ltd, the state-owned news company, provides the news content for both television and radio. It also runs all current affairs and talk show programmes on television.

2.1   General programming

Television

ZTV, the television arm of the ZBC, is responsible for children's, youth and educational programmes, as well as cartoons, lifestyle shows, music programmes, soaps and drama.

With regard to all these programme genres other than news and current affairs, there was initially hope that the introduction of the local content policy in 2001 would expand the choice of formats and offerings generally. The Broadcasting Services Act stipulates in its Sixth Schedule that 40 per cent of the content offered by the state broadcaster must be commissioned from independent producers. The audio-visual industry in the country blossomed for a brief period with the emergence of a number of local productions, notably two popular soaps, *Studio 263* and *Makorokoza,* as well as a series of other local dramas and comedies. However, due to fiscal constraints within the broadcaster and the economy as a whole, quality local productions dwindled and the ZBC began to rely more and more on repeats. Although the Broadcasting Services Act stipulates that 40 per cent of the content must be commissioned from independent producers, by early 2009 the ZBC obtained only 10 per cent of its programming from that source.[74]

The BSA provides for a Broadcasting Fund which is supposed to encourage the growth of the creative arts industries. However, by mid-2009, eight years after the promulgation of the law, this fund had still not been put in place. Over the years, local producers have also expressed concern that the ZBC is 'political' in its commissioning and selection of programmes. These concerns were, for instance, raised in the 2004 *Second Report of the Portfolio Committee on Transport and Communication on Zimbabwe Broadcasting Holdings,* which established that:

> ... the selection of material from production houses had rather been biased; implying that production houses that did not hold favour with the broadcaster had found their works rejected ... Many documentaries which had been accepted regionally and internationally had been rejected by the public broadcaster. It was further submitted that in certain instances there was content manipulation in the selection methods and this had largely been on political grounds.[75]

This and other reports of the portfolio committee, however, did not have any measurable impact on the ZBC's programming.

In a typical week (18 to 24 May 2009) locally produced news and current affairs make up the largest chunk of programming on ZTV's schedule (from 06h00 to 00h30) – with a total of three-and-a-half hours per weekday (plus 90 minutes of repeats), including one hour (at 17h30) in Shona and Ndebele. On average 60 minutes per day are dedicated to (foreign) documentaries (half an hour each), including repeats.

There is a one-hour talk show once a week (Fridays 22h00 with a repeat on Tuesdays) called *Amai Chisamba* ('Amai' in Shona means mother and Chisamba stands for the name of the host, Rebecca Chisamba), which usually deals with 'safe' subjects focusing on Zimbabwean families and communities. Expressing criticism can result in harsh retributive action. For instance, on 16 June 2007 the show broadcast a programme on women and children who were survivors of rape and child sexual abuse, with the director of the Girl Child Network, Betty Makoni, as a guest. She brought along girls being sheltered at her organisation, whose faces were electronically blurred, to narrate their experiences. The Network has been at the forefront of exposing rape abuses perpetrated by ZANU PF militias and other sexual abuses by those in positions of power. As a result, the organisation and its director have on several occasions been

---

74 Interviews with Walter Mufanochiya, ZBH scheduling manager, 25 April 2008 and 20 March 2009.
75 Parliament of Zimbabwe, 2004:7, cited in D. Moyo, *Broadcasting Policy Reform and Democratisation in Zambia and Zimbabwe, 1990-2005: Global Pressures, National Responses.* UniPub: Oslo, 2006.

targeted by the police. The screening of this programme led to the arrest of both Betty Makoni and the host of the show.[76]

Thirty-minute soaps and dramas make up one-and-a-half hours of a weekday's programming. Most of these are old foreign-produced programmes, such as *Keeping up Appearances* (UK), *Jewel in the Korean Palace* (Korea) and *Suburban Bliss* (South Africa), often repeated the following day. A local drama is broadcast weekdays from 19h30 to 20h00. On average half an hour per day each is dedicated to music shows and lifestyle programmes (mainly cooking shows). Children are offered various 30-minute slots over the week (foreign and local productions) and a two-hour show, *Star Kidz*, on Saturday mornings.

As prescribed by the Broadcasting Services Act the ZBC is obliged to cover all 'national events', frequently resulting in sudden changes to the programme schedule. Such events include, for example, funerals of 'heroes' (senior ZANU PF stalwarts) at the Heroes Acre, ZANU PF conferences and presidential trips abroad. The Act also requires the ZBC to make a total of one hour per week of its broadcasting time on each of its channels available for the purpose of enabling the government to explain its mandate to the nation. The effect of these requirements has been a disproportional amount of broadcasting time allocated to programmes dealing with ZANU PF events and political campaigning activities at the expense of a diversity of other happenings (non-state events, civil society activities, opposition party events) which might be similarly regarded as being of 'national' importance.

In June 2009, the ZBC announced that it had concluded an agreement with a South African company, Fairmead Consultants, to acquire 104 children's programmes, 130 assorted documentaries, 156 family movies, 52 karate movies, 100 filler programmes (unspecified) and 52 lifestyle magazine programmes.[77] The scheduling manager, Walter Mufanochiya, stated:

> We have received the first lot of programmes we secured from Fairmead and we hope that these will go a long way in turning around the fortunes of the broadcaster. The past few years have been difficult, mainly because we did not have any foreign currency to buy programmes, but we are back now and we intend to reclaim our viewers ... We also want to assure our viewers that ZTV is taking a turn for the better and from now onwards, things are going to be improving.

---

76 The two were arrested ostensibly for violating section 197 of the Criminal Procedures and Evidence Act by revealing the identities of under-age girls, despite the fact that their faces were hidden.
77 'ZBC-TV unveils new programmes regime', *The Sunday Mail*, 28 June 2009, at http://www.sundaymail.co.zw/inside.aspx?sectid=2823&cat=3, accessed 29 June 2009.

It is not quite clear how two more children's programmes, three more movies or one more lifestyle magazine a week – all of them foreign productions – are supposed to result in a genuine turnaround for the broadcaster.

Radio

Radio Zimbabwe was originally established under the name Radio 4 to offer development programmes, using the two country's main languages Shona and Ndbele, and to give different groups a platform to air their views. It was best known for promoting and broadcasting a project called Development Through Radio (DTR), initiated and managed by the Federation of African Media Women Zimbabwe (FAMWZ). The project created radio listening clubs involving rural women who would gather to listen to programmes by and about themselves. It was hoped that opinion leaders would emerge from the radio listening clubs who would then relay this development information to others. These days Radio Zimbabwe is mainly a music station with five-minute news on the hour from 06h00 to 23h00 and four 20-minute news bulletins a day. Special 55-minute programmes are offered daily for women, the youth and children. Brief talk segments (15 to 30 minutes) are broadcast three times a day. Occasionally the station sells air time to NGOs, for example to the Farm Community Trust of Zimbabwe (FCTZ) to transmit its 15-minute programme *Upfumi Kuwanhu* (literally translated 'Wealth to the People') every Tuesday. These programmes are broadcast during prime time from 18h45 to 19h00.

Spot FM targets 'mature', middle-class audiences and broadcasts in English. The station has a three-minute headline news service on the hour from 06h00 to 24h00 and a half-hour bulletin at 13h00 and 18h00. Its programme schedule follows a traditional pattern of 30-minute slots interspersed with music. Spot FM offers six talk shows per day discussing mainly entertainment and lifestyle topics, sports information and half-hour programmes such as *Book Review, The Nationalist Leader, Wheels of Justice, Women in Business, Business Talk* and the like. From 11h03 to 12h00 Spot FM broadcasts a regular women's programme.

Power FM is a youth radio station broadcasting mainly in English. The station offers music almost exclusively, some of it in the form of requests, plus half an hour of birthday greetings, 15 minutes of sports and a five-minute quiz a day. Five minutes of news are broadcast nine times a day.

National FM focuses on social and developmental issues and broadcasts in 17 languages.

2.2 News

A special report was commissioned for this survey from the Media Monitoring Project of Zimbabwe (MMPZ)[78] to assess news and current affairs programmes aired on the ZBC and two of the foreign-based, Zimbabwean-run private radio stations (SW Radio Africa and Studio 7) for a three-week period between 13 July and 2 August 2009.

Obviously, this is a comparison between two very different outputs, in respect of purpose as well as volume. The foreign-based stations were set up with the express intention to provide an alternative to the information disseminated by the government via the state broadcaster and to give a platform to those whose voices were habitually excluded from it. And while the ZBC runs a round-the-clock service with a large number of regular news slots providing extensive space for whatever it wants to put across, the private stations are on air for a couple of hours a day only, and thus need to make very careful choices. Nevertheless, comparing the two does help to show up more clearly how partial the state broadcaster's coverage of what is happening in the country (and beyond) on a day-to-day basis really is – both in terms of selection and treatment.

ZBC news coverage focused on socio-economic issues which featured in 31.2 per cent of stories broadcast during the period under review, followed by stories on the inclusive government (20 per cent) and news about communities and development (9.3 per cent). The private stations, on the other hand, put more emphasis on human rights issues (17.6 per cent of stories) and the debate surrounding the development of a new constitution for Zimbabwe (16 per cent). By comparison, only 8 per cent of ZBC stories dealt with the constitutional debate and 0.8 per cent with human rights issues. Twenty-four per cent of stories on private stations reported on the inclusive government and 16.8 per cent covered socio-economic issues.

The distribution of sources follows a similarly distinctive pattern. The main sources used by the ZBC were government (11.9 per cent), MDC ministers (13.2 per cent) and ZANU PF ministers (11.6 per cent). While the ZBC quoted the ZANU PF party in 9.8 per cent of its stories, statements from the two MDC formations were included in only 4 per cent. The private radios quoted MDC sources in 16.2 per cent of their stories and ZANU PF in only 1.4 per cent. The main sources of information for the private stations (37.3 per cent) are 'alternative' voices, that is, civil society representatives, and 'legal voices' (9.9 per cent).

This assessment of ZBC news bulletins during the period under review shows

---

78 *A comparative analysis of ZBC and private radio stations' coverage of issues: July 13th–August 2nd 2009.* Report compiled by the MMPZ during September 2009.

that in party-political terms – on the face of it – the broadcaster seemingly provides 'balanced' news, even giving 'preference' to MDC ministers. A closer look reveals a somewhat different picture. The weeks examined here saw the start of national conferences to review Zimbabwe's constitution and the launch of 'national peace days' promoting national reconciliation. On many of these occasions MDC officials 'were mainly cited in the context of reinforcing the notion of a united government' – quotes that conveyed a message which is in the interest of ZANU PF.[79]

None of the ZBC's stories on the inclusive government 'openly exposed the tensions in the new government and their effects on its stability.' According to the MMPZ, government officials quoted were 'depicting it as united and focused on the source of the country's problems and the requisite solutions.' In contrast, most of the private stations' stories on the inclusive government 'cited analysts noting the problems plaguing the coalition since its inception, which they mainly traced to ZANU PF's disdain for the global political agreement.'

In July and August 2009 several MDC members of parliament were prosecuted and convicted of what were described as trumped up charges (such as the alleged theft of a cell phone) and consequently suspended from the national assembly – the widely suspected purpose being to reduce or wipe out the slight MDC majority in the house. In the weeks monitored there was no mention of such suspensions and their implications on ZBC channels.

During the same period Prime Minister Tsvangirai called upon then SADC Chairman and President of South Africa Jacob Zuma to intervene against 'unilateral decisions' by President Mugabe – again without any coverage by the state broadcaster.

When the first day of a national constitutional conference descended into chaos created by ZANU PF supporters, ZTV news featured an 'analyst' who explained the party's actions as agitation for a 'home-grown constitution amid revelations that there was an external hand in the process' (without substantiating his claims) – the 'analyst' was ZANU PF Governor Martin Dinha.

Continuing human rights violations against MDC members and supporters remain largely unreported by the state broadcaster. High profile arrests or court appearances are either not reflected in the news at all or rate a mere mention among other general crime or court cases. 'The private radio stations carried 20 stories on alleged human rights abuses as compared to six featured on ZBC. The private radio stations recorded six new alleged incidents of rights abuses. The ZBC ignored these reports.'

On closer examination it becomes clear that ZBC news broadcasts are used as partisan instruments to shore up the position of ZANU PF in the inclusive government

---

79 MMPZ *Weekly Reports* 2009-29, 20–26 July 2009.

and to project an image of the party still being largely in charge. The constant reference to President Mugabe as 'Head of State and Government and Commander-in-chief of the Defence Forces' ignores the power-sharing provisions [of the agreement between the parties] by promoting the idea of Mugabe as having a monopoly on executive power in the unity government'[80] – with little mention of the fact that he shares this power with the MDC's Morgan Tsvangirai as prime minister.

Titles and modes of address used in ZBC news have long been indicative of the stance of the broadcaster and continue to be so. MDC members of government are habitually referred to as 'Mr' and 'Mrs' in the bulletins, while ZANU PF officials are always 'Comrade' – a term that denotes membership in the party of liberation and the ranks of anti-colonial struggle heroes. Not according this honorific to members of other parties subtly suggests that they played no role in this struggle.

2.3 Current affairs

The MMPZ in its report for this survey notes that the ZBC's current affairs programmes 'generally offered a diversified and more measured assessment of the country's political and socio-economic evolution' than its news coverage.

In a specific focus on some of ZTV's current affairs programmes, the MMPZ found that two of them (*The Legislator* and *Face The Nation*) included a range of opinions on the topics discussed, while three (*The Melting Pot*, *Madzindza* and *Media Watch*) were essentially used to reflect and reinforce ZANU PF views. The programme *Talking Farming* basically aims at building the knowledge of resettled indigenous farmers in terms of Zimbabwe's land distribution policies.

On radio, the ZBC's Spot FM devoted 45 minutes every working day (Monday to Friday) between 09h15 and 10h00 to STERP, the government's Short Term Emergency Recovery Programme of March 2009. 'However, almost all the programmes turned out to be bland public relations platforms for the coalition that lacked critical examination of its programmes.'

In the period under review and 'as has become the norm ahead of the country's annual Heroes Day commemorations [on 11 August], the station punctuated its programming with *Heroes/National Events* slots every Monday to Friday between 10 am and 2pm and in the evening between 6pm and 10pm. The programmes profiled the lives and contributions of the late nationalists to the country's struggle for independence.'

In contrast, according to the MMPZ report, SW Radio Africa's current affairs slots

---

80 Ibid., 2009-30, 27 July–2 August 2009.

9
Broadcasting Reform Efforts

1　Background

Media reform has been on the agenda in Zimbabwe for more than a decade and the debate intensified after the promulgation of the highly contested Broadcasting Services Act in 2001. Reform efforts and initiatives have been spearheaded by various media advocacy groups, in particular the Zimbabwe national chapter of the Media Institute of Southern Africa (MISA-Zimbabwe), the Media Monitoring Project of Zimbabwe (MMPZ) and the Zimbabwe Union of Journalists (ZUJ).

The MMPZ conducts detailed monitoring of especially news and current affairs content of all the major media in the country (state and privately-owned, print and electronic, including the radio broadcasts of Zimbabwean stations operating from abroad) and publishes weekly reports. The aim is to gauge – both quantitatively and qualitatively – how the voices of political parties and civil society are being represented and reflected in the country's media. The project also publishes special reports covering each election period as well as thematic reports focusing on specific topics from time to time.

The MMPZ also does rural outreach and advocacy work on media law reform through its Public Information Rights Forum (PIRF). It has established a dozen PIRF committees in various districts of the country, bringing together teachers, health workers, students, community activists and ordinary citizens who disseminate and discuss the work and findings of the MMPZ and lobby for media law reform within their own communities. Other innovative MMPZ projects have included the staging of a play in the form of guerrilla theatre, performed without notice and on the spot 76 times in outlying towns and rural areas in all provinces of the country in late 2007 and early 2008. The play addressed the subject of constitutional reform and reached an estimated 11 000 spectators.[81]

MISA-Zimbabwe, which has led the struggle for media law reform in the country, began actively advocating for broadcasting reform in 1998 under the 'Free the Airwaves Campaign' initiated and organised by the regional secretariat of the Institute. The campaign in Zimbabwe focused mainly on the need for an independent regulatory authority, the transformation of the ZBC into a genuine public service broadcaster and the opening up of the airwaves to allow other players to enter the broadcasting sector. Between 2001 and 2004, MISA-Zimbabwe, together with other media groups, held conferences and seminars, ran adverts and also hired drama groups which travelled around the country in order to promote these goals.

MISA-Zimbabwe has long placed special emphasis on promoting community broadcasting by setting up advocacy committees made up of media and community activists in seven centres countrywide. The purpose has been to engage communities about the concept of community radio and how such stations function as a critical component of development as well as participatory democracy. These committees have been the platform for the establishment of the Zimbabwean Association of Community Radio Stations (ZACRAS) – which operates under the auspices of MISA-Zimbabwe – and which is now lobbying for the opening up of the airwaves to non-state community broadcasters.

To strengthen their lobbying power MISA, the MMPZ and ZUJ together with the Zimbabwe National Editors' Forum (ZINEF) formed the Media Alliance of Zimbabwe (MAZ) in 2004. ZINEF is a forum of editors of non-state media (broadcast, online and print, publishing or broadcasting both inside and outside the country). For specific activities the MAZ cooperates with a range of other media associations and NGOs such as the Federation of African Media Women Zimbabwe (FAMWZ), the Zimbabwe Association of Community Radio Stations (ZACRAS), Kubatana (an Internet, mobile and print-based communication platform for civil society organisations) and the African Community Publishing and Development Trust (ACPD). The ACPD aims to promote peace-building and strengthen human rights, governance and democracy in Zimbabwe by working directly with dozens of community groups in virtually every district and in all the languages spoken in the country.

From its inception the alliance and its partners have been lobbying for media law reform and broadcasting reform in particular. Their campaigns target the public at

---

81   Evaluation Report of the MMPZ by Jeanette Minnie submitted to OSISA on 29 March 2009.

communities in outlying towns and rural areas, other civil society organisations
ıuman rights networks.

ınce 2004, advocacy for media reform has increasingly taken place at regional
continental levels. MISA-Zimbabwe, the MMPZ and ZUJ in conjunction with a
.ıumber of human rights organisations have lobbied continental and regional bodies
such as the African Union's Commission for Human and Peoples' Rights and the
Southern African Development Community (SADC). This lobbying has contributed
to pressure building up on the government of Zimbabwe from among its peers on
the continent and incrementally played a significant role in helping to bring about
amendments of the Broadcasting Services Act and the Access to Information and
Privacy Act (AIPPA) in December 2007.

2 Current reform efforts

A conference under the title 'Media Legislation in Zimbabwe: Now is the time to
act' held in Johannesburg, South Africa in August 2008, initiated a broad-based
Campaign for Media Reform to be coordinated by MAZ, with MISA-Zimbabwe as
the lead agency. This decision was taken just before the conclusion of the Global
Political Agreement between ZANU PF and the two MDC formations in the
following month, which led to the establishment of the inclusive government in
February 2009.

Because the conference in Johannesburg was attended only by a core group of
representatives of key non-state media organisations and media lobby groups, MAZ
decided to hold a broader second consultative conference in Harare in December
2008. 'The Media We Want: Free, Fair and Open' attracted a larger number of media
practitioners and activists as well as representatives from outlying towns and districts
in the country.

A notable result from these two conferences was a follow-up strategic planning
meeting in January 2009 initiated by the MAZ which established the Media Legal
Reform Committee consisting of Zimbabwean media and human rights lawyers and
two international advisors.

In regard to broadcasting reform, the Committee decided to focus on the creation
of an independent broadcasting regulator and the transformation of the ZBC into a
public broadcaster. To this end the Committee drafted a Framework for a New Media
Policy and a Zimbabwe Broadcasting Corporation bill. At the time of writing the
Committee was working on a bill for an independent broadcasting regulator.

All these documents follow international standards and best practices. They also draw on the findings of this survey, which were put at the reform committee's disposal as soon as the relevant draft chapters had been completed.

The inclusive government committed itself to media reforms in the Global Political Agreement of September 2008 but concrete efforts towards the achievement of this aim were slow to get off the ground. In May 2009 the government issued an invitation to a stakeholders' conference on media reforms. This was boycotted, however, by a large section of the media and many of the organisations mentioned above. They were suspicious of the agenda informed by ZANU PF philosophy and the list of speakers dominated by ZANU PF stalwarts. They also doubted the government's genuine commitment to meaningful media reforms, given a new spate of human rights violations that had begun in December 2008 involving raids on various NGOs and the abduction, arrest and torture of journalists and human rights activists over the following months.

Shortly after the government conference, parliament called for applications for membership of the Zimbabwe Media Commission (ZMC) provided for in the amended constitution to licence newspapers, among other things. MISA-Zimbabwe and the MMPZ are opposed to this kind of regulation of the media and maintain that publications do not need statutory licensing. However, the two organisations found themselves caught in a tactical dilemma: as the law stands, the ZMC is a fact of life and no new paper would be able enter the market legally without being given the go-ahead by the Commission. A boycott of the selection process would have meant sticking to a principled position, but at the same time being seen as standing in the way of a more pluralistic media landscape. In the end, the two organisations issued a statement protesting against the move – and silently accepted the process.

The parliamentary Committee on Standing Rules and Orders, in charge of selecting the members of constitutional commissions, duly interviewed candidates for the ZMC in August 2009. A list of 12 names was passed on to President Mugabe for him to choose and appoint nine of these persons as commissioners.

In an unexpected move the parliamentary committee also drew up a list of names for the board of the Broadcasting Authority of Zimbabwe (BAZ) (in charge of licensing broadcasters) at the same time and from the same pool of ZMC nominations – without any previous announcement or tender or asking nominees if they were prepared to serve on the BAZ. Media advocacy and human rights groups protested and stated that parliament had prejudiced prospective candidates for the Broadcasting Authority. They pointed out that the selection processes for the two organisations are governed by separate legal provisions and should, therefore, have been conducted separately.

On 30 September 2009, Minister of Media, Information and Publicity Webster

Shamu nevertheless appointed a new BAZ, with most of its members having been drawn from the ZMC nomination pool.

At the same time the minister announced his appointments to various parastatals and other organisations which he regards as falling under his ministry: Zimbabwe Broadcasting Corporation, Zimpapers, New Ziana, Transmedia and Kingstons (a booksellers, stationers and newsagents chain). The MDC complained that it had not been consulted and promised that the decisions would be reviewed.

Media lobby and other civil society groups strongly condemned the appointments which, they said, 'turn the clock back in terms of reforms'.[82] The fact that a total of nine retired senior military officials are among the board members (two for the BAZ, three for the ZBC, one each for Zimpapers, Transmedia, Kingstons and New Ziana) was described as 'extremely disturbing' and having the 'potential for the militarisation of the media at a time when it should be democratised'.[83]

Media lobby groups have involved themselves in the development of a new constitution, an undertaking which tops the agenda of the inclusive government. The MAZ's Framework for a New Media Policy demands that 'the freedom of expression guarantee in the new constitution should include express guarantees of media freedom, access to information, freedom of artistic creativity and academic freedom' and that 'any restrictions on the right to freedom of expression should be provided for by law, serve a legitimate interest and be necessary in a democratic society.'[84]

The call for media reform and the transformation of the ZBC into a public broadcaster enjoys broad in-principle support in civil society, among others from organisations such as the Zimbabwe Election Support Network (ZESN), the Crisis in Zimbabwe Coalition (CZC) and the National Constitutional Assembly (NCA). The ZESN is a coalition of 36 Zimbabwean NGOs formed to coordinate activities pertaining to elections, and to promote democratic processes in general and free and fair elections in particular.[85] The CZC, which consists of 300 civic groups, is a collective response to the multi-faceted crisis facing the nation. Its mandate broadly covers socio-economic and political issues.[86] The NCA is a conglomerate of human rights organisations, churches, trade unions, women's groups, professionals and interested individuals that pushes for a people-driven constitution for Zimbabwe.[87]

In interviews for this survey,[88] representatives of these and other groups agreed that the ZBC has failed the people of Zimbabwe by operating as a 'party' broadcaster that

82 Ernest Mudzengi, coordinator of the National Constitutional Assembly NGO, quoted in *Zimbabwe Independent*, 2 October 2009.
83 MISA-Zimbabwe press statement 2 October 2009.
84 Media Framework Policy for Zimbabwe, MAZ Working Paper, Harare, June 2009.
85 http://www.zesn.org.zw/default.cfm?pid=1
86 http://www.crisiszimbabwe.org/?q=node/10
87 http://www.cbrc.org.za/Civcom_NCA.htm
88 Interviews took place through emails between 20 July and 18 August 2009.

only serves the interests of ZANU PF. The groups were similarly unanimous in their demand for the transformation of the ZBC into a truly public broadcaster through a new broadcasting law and a constitutional guarantee for its independence.

So far, however, these organisations – and others such as churches, the Consumer Council of Zimbabwe and the Zimbabwe Congress of Trade Unions – have not been actively involved in what was envisaged as a 'broad-based' campaign in August 2008. Broadcasting reforms have traditionally been, and still are, the preserve of media-oriented organisations, specifically MISA-Zimbabwe and the MMPZ. As a result media law reform advocacy tends to remain trapped as a demand from the non-state media sector in Zimbabwe, instead of one actively pursued by society as a whole. There is still too little understanding among the general public of the dynamics and the far-reaching effects of broadcasting policy and regulatory issues on the health and vibrancy of a democratic society.

3   Conclusion and recommendations

The deeply unsatisfactory state of affairs in regard to broadcasting in general and the Zimbabwe Broadcasting Corporation in particular should be fertile ground for campaigns and concerted efforts in support of fundamental reform of the political and legal foundations for this sector. The inclusive government, however, seems to be a reluctant player in this regard and displays no sense of urgency especially when it comes to the ZBC. This is understandable as far as ZANU PF is concerned, because the broadcaster in its present shape greatly strengthens its hand. It is puzzling, however, why the MDC should not have pushed more forcefully for drastic change at the ZBC from the inception of the new government.

Media advocacy groups need to increase pressure on the government by:

- More actively involving other civil society groups such as churches, trade unions and human rights organisations in their campaigns, with the aim to really bring about a broad-based coalition for media reforms as envisaged in August 2008;
- Widely publishing policy papers developed by MAZ such as the Media Policy Framework, the ZBC Bill and other documents in English, Shona and Ndebele;
- Lobbying political parties, especially their core leadership, on the essentials of a democratic broadcasting reform;
- Submitting policy papers developed by MAZ, such as the Media Policy

Framework, to the Thematic Commission of the Constitutional Reform Process in charge of media issues;

- Encouraging and assisting members of parliament to submit private member bills in regard to broadcasting and other media reforms;
- Initiating panel discussions on broadcasting issues throughout the country;
- Urging the ZBC to allow free debate on the future of the organisation on its airwaves;
- Intensifying campaigns throughout the country, among others through activities run by the MMPZ's Public Information Rights Forum, the Advocacy Committees of MISA-Zimbabwe and the members of ZACRAS;
- Using creative ways of informing the public on the aims and importance of broadcasting reform, such as drama performances;
- Linking up with the African Community Publishing and Development Trust (ACPD), which operates in rural districts and communities, to extend the scope of the campaign.

10
Recommendations

1 Constitution

Section 20 of the present constitution does not sufficiently guarantee freedom of expression, including freedom of the media. The debate on a new section in this regard in a new constitution should be guided by the Declaration of Principles on Freedom of Expression in Africa of the African Commission on Human and Peoples' Rights (2002), which states:

> Freedom of expression and information, including the right to seek, receive and impart information and ideas, either orally, in writing or in print, in the form of art, or through any other form of communication, including across frontiers, is a fundamental and inalienable human right and an indispensable component of democracy.
> Everyone shall have an equal opportunity to exercise the right to freedom of expression and to access information without discrimination.

2 Media laws in general

- Laws inhibiting the free operations of the media must be repealed without delay. The most important of these is the Access to Information and Protection of Privacy Act (AIPPA).
- A statutory commission for the regulation of the media has no place in a democratic state. The provision in the Constitutional Amendment 19 of

February 2009 to set up a Zimbabwe Media Commission must be scrapped during the constitutional review process.

- The Public Order and Security Act (POSA) which, in conjunction with AIPPA, severely limits the right of the media to freedom of expression, must be repealed without delay and replaced with legislation appropriate for a democratic state.
- There is no need for general media-specific legislation or a specific registration law – publishing companies are subject to the Companies Act like every other enterprise.
- All laws that might curtail or have an impact on freedom of expression (such as secrecy laws) need to be reviewed and – where necessary – amended.

3   Access to information

Currently, access by the public to information held by government authorities is regulated by the Access to Information and Protection of Privacy Act (AIPPA). This Act needs to be repealed in its entirety and a new access to information law should be passed. The guidelines set by the Declaration of Principles on Freedom of Expression in Africa provide a good model to be followed:

1) Public bodies hold information not for themselves but as custodians of the public good and everyone has a right to access this information, subject only to clearly defined rules established by law.
2) The right to information shall be guaranteed by law in accordance with the following principles:
   i)   everyone has the right to access information held by public bodies;
   ii) everyone has the right to access information held by private bodies which is necessary for the exercise or protection of any right;
   iii) any refusal to disclose information shall be subject to appeal to an independent body and/or the courts;
   iv) public bodies shall be required, even in the absence of a request, actively to publish important information of significant public interest;
   v)   no one shall be subject to any sanction for releasing in good faith information on wrongdoing, or that which would disclose a serious threat to health, safety or the environment save where the imposition of sanctions serves a legitimate interest and is necessary in a democratic society; and

vi) secrecy laws shall be amended as necessary to comply with freedom of information principles.

..e right of access to information should be included in the Constitution.

4 Voluntary Media Council of Zimbabwe

The Voluntary Media Council needs to be strengthened by:

- Ensuring that the Council represents all the media in the country. To this end editors of state-controlled media must be encouraged to join the body;
- Embarking on a comprehensive public relations campaign to make readers, listeners and viewers of the media aware of the existence of a complaints body.

5 Broadcasting landscape

- The Broadcasting Authority of Zimbabwe (BAZ) should issue broadcasting licences to commercial and community broadcasters so that a three-tier broadcasting system is realised.
- The state-owned signal company, TransMedia, should be supervised by the Broadcasting Authority of Zimbabwe (once a new Broadcasting Services Act is in place). It should be restructured to enable it to deal effectively with transmission problems facing the national broadcaster and to meet the challenges posed by digitalisation.
- The Broadcasting Services Act must allow for more than one additional signal carrier company and for commercial/community broadcasting services to operate their own transmitter network if they wish.

6 Digitalisation

A policy for digital migration should be produced as a matter of urgency. Steps need to be taken to:

- Establish a Digital Migration Taskforce to draw up a Digital Broadcasting

Migration Paper for Zimbabwe;
* Launch a consumer education and awareness campaign to inform the public about the digital migration process;
* Launch a Green/White Paper process to assess the implications of Zimbabwe adopting a law on the convergence of broadcasting and telecommunications and the pros and cons of a converged regulator.

7   Broadcasting legislation

* The Broadcasting Services Act should be reviewed in its entirety and replaced as a matter of urgency by a new broadcasting regulatory law with the aim of creating an independent broadcasting authority. The independence of this authority should be guaranteed in the new constitution.
* Broadcasting and telecommunications regulation should remain separate so that an independent broadcasting regulator can focus on the development of a diverse, vibrant and sustainable broadcasting industry in the country.
* The local content policy should be subjected to thorough debate throughout the country and the new independent broadcasting regulator should call for position papers from interested stakeholders. Realistic and achievable local content quotas should then be set, which will not have the effect of insulating Zimbabwe from global news, views and knowledge while at the same time boosting local production and quality content.
* The public complaints system for broadcasting should be reviewed and established in accordance with Clause 9 of the Declaration of Principles on Freedom of Expression in Africa which states:

1)   A public complaints system for print or broadcasting should be available in accordance with the following principles:
    i)   complaints shall be determined in accordance with established rules and codes of conduct agreed between all stakeholders; and
    ii)   the complaints system shall be widely accessible.

2)   Any regulatory body established to hear complaints about media content, including media councils, shall be protected against political, economic or any other undue interference. Its powers shall be administrative in nature and it shall not seek to usurp the role of the courts.

3)   Effective self-regulation is the best system for promoting high standards in the media.

- Submitting these documents to the Thematic Commission of the Constitutional Reform Process in charge of media issues;
- Lobbying political parties, especially their core leadership, on the essentials of a democratic broadcasting reform;
- Encouraging and assisting members of parliament to submit private member bills in regard to broadcasting and other media reforms;
- Initiating panel discussions on broadcasting issues throughout the country;
- Urging the ZBC to allow free debate on the future of the organisation on its airwaves.

AfriMAP, the Africa Governance Monitoring and Advocacy Project, is an initiative of the Soros foundation network's four African foundations, and works with national civil society organisations to conduct systematic audits of government performance in three areas: the justice sector and the rule of law; political participation and democracy; and effective delivery of public services.
www.afrimap.org

The Open Society Institute works to build vibrant and tolerant democracies whose governments are accountable to their citizens. To achieve its mission, OSI seeks to shape public policies that assure greater fairness in political, legal, and economic systems and safeguard fundamental rights. At a local level, OSI implements a range of initiatives to advance justice, education, public health, and independent media. At the same time, OSI builds alliances across borders and continents on issues such as corruption and freedom of information. OSI places a high priority on protecting and improving the lives of people in marginalised communities.
www.soros.org

It is recommended therefore that the complaints system for broadcasting should be the responsibility of the Voluntary Media Council of Zimbabwe.

8   The Zimbabwe Broadcasting Corporation (ZBC): Legislation

- A ZBC Act must be passed to transform the present state broadcaster into a public broadcaster that serves the public interest as a matter of urgency. The Act must outline clear governing structures which shield the broadcaster from political interference and interference from other powerful forces in society that seek to influence it unduly.
- The ZBC should be governed by a board established and acting according to the following principles:
  - Appointment procedures should be open, transparent and free from political interference.
  - The board should represent a broad cross-section of the Zimbabwean population.
  - Persons who are office bearers with the state or political parties or have business interests in the media industry should not be eligible for board membership.
  - Its role should be clearly set out in law and its main responsibility should be to ensure that the public broadcaster is protected against undue political or commercial influences and fulfils its mandate in the public interest.
  - It should not interfere in the day-to-day decision-making of the broadcaster especially in relation to broadcast content and respect the principle of editorial independence.
- The new ZBC Act should guarantee editorial independence for the ZBC.
- Management and journalists at the ZBC need training on the concept of public broadcasting, focusing on:
  - principles and values of public broadcasting;
  - the role of journalists and management in a public broadcaster;
  - challenges facing public broadcasters in the era of commercialisation and competition; and
  - the role of public broadcasting in the digital era.

9   The Zimbabwe Broadcasting Corporation (ZBC): Funding

The basic precondition for any successful reform of funding is the passing and implementation of a new ZBC Act, that is, the transformation of the state into a credible public broadcaster offering quality programming designed to meet diverse audience needs.

In view of the present financial status of the ZBC it is recommended that:

- The new board commission a thorough audit of the Corporation's financial status by an independent accounting firm;
- On the basis of a new programme policy the organisational structure of the ZBC be reviewed and reformed, in particular regarding administrative processes and expenses;
- On the basis of the new programme policy and organisational structure, a business plan be developed which reflects the financial needs of the ZBC and potential sources of revenue.

The ZBC should be funded through a mix of licence fees, revenues from the state fiscus and advertisements/sponsorships.

Regarding licence fees it is recommended that:

- Licence fees form the backbone of the ZBC's revenue sources because they provide stable, predictable multi-year funding and allow the broadcaster to plan and implement the necessary investment in programming and operational improvements;
- The amount of licence fees be fair and socially/economically justifiable;
- Households in regions not covered by ZBC signals not be required to pay licence fees;
- Efforts be made to improve significantly the compliance rate for payment of the fee among viewers and listeners.

In regard to revenues from the state fiscus, it is recommended that:

- An independent panel of experts determine the amount of a subsidy needed by the ZBC over a three-year period to fulfill its public broadcasting mandate;
- Parliament fund the public broadcaster directly (and not through a ministry or department) on the basis of the amount determined by the panel of experts.

Concerning advertisements and sponsorships it is recommended that:

- The ZBC develop clear and strict guidelines on soliciting advertisements and conditions for accepting advertisements and programme sponsorships that will safeguard the broadcaster's editorial independence and clearly separate the responsibilities of editorial and marketing departments;
- The new broadcasting regulator embarks on a process of public consultation with the objective to set appropriate limits to advertising and sponsorship on ZBC.

10 The Zimbabwe Broadcasting Corporation (ZBC): Programming

On the basis of new legislation for the ZBC, the broadcaster should:

- In a process of public consultation, develop a programme charter that adheres to public broadcasting principles and promotes public interest programming;
- Develop a code of conduct and establish an effective internal complaints mechanism through which citizens can express their concerns about content that they find inappropriate or unacceptable;
- Consult widely with stakeholders and the public at large to develop an appropriate local content policy;
- Develop a professional and mutually beneficial relationship with local audio-visual production companies;
- Set up a commissioning unit that will ensure diversity of output.

11 Campaigns for broadcasting reforms

Media advocacy groups need to increase pressure on the government by:

- More actively involving other civil society groups such as churches, trade unions and human rights organisations in their campaigns, with the aim to really bring about a broad-based coalition for media reforms as envisaged in August 2008;
- Widely publishing policy papers developed by the Media Alliance of Zimbabwe such as the Media Policy Framework, the ZBC Bill and other documents in English, Shona and Ndebele;

www.ingramcontent.com/pod-product-compliance
Lightning Source LLC
Chambersburg PA
CBHW081741270326
41932CB00020B/3355